# Distributed Serverless Architectures on AWS

## Design and Implement Serverless Architectures

Jithin Jude Paul

Apress®

***Distributed Serverless Architectures on AWS: Design and Implement Serverless Architectures***

Jithin Jude Paul
Ernakulam, Kerala, India

ISBN-13 (pbk): 978-1-4842-9158-0 ISBN-13 (electronic): 978-1-4842-9159-7
https://doi.org/10.1007/978-1-4842-9159-7



Managing Director, Apress Media LLC: Welmoed Spahr
Acquisitions Editor: Celestin Suresh John
Development Editor: James Markham
Coordinating Editor: Shrikant Vishwakarma
Copy Editor: Kim Wimpsett

Cover designed by eStudioCalamar

Cover image by Scott Webb on Unsplash (www.unsplash.com)

Distributed to the book trade worldwide by Apress Media, LLC, 1 New York Plaza, New York, NY 10004, U.S.A. Phone 1-800-SPRINGER, fax (201) 348-4505, e-mail orders-ny@springer-sbm.com, or visit www.springeronline.com. Apress Media, LLC is a California LLC and the sole member (owner) is Springer Science + Business Media Finance Inc (SSBM Finance Inc). SSBM Finance Inc is a **Delaware** corporation.

For information on translations, please e-mail booktranslations@springernature.com; for reprint, paperback, or audio rights, please e-mail bookpermissions@springernature.com.

Apress titles may be purchased in bulk for academic, corporate, or promotional use. eBook versions and licenses are also available for most titles. For more information, reference our Print and eBook Bulk Sales web page at http://www.apress.com/bulk-sales.

Any source code or other supplementary material referenced by the author in this book is available to readers on GitHub (https://github.com/Apress). For more detailed information, please visit http://www.apress.com/source-code.

Printed on acid-free paper

*First and foremost, I dedicate this book to my wife Chanthini, because without her constant support I would not have been able to complete it. She managed our kids and our home, without complaining, as I spent numerous hours writing this book.*

*I also dedicate this book to my daughters, Norah and Amelia, who missed out on their playtime with me, while I engrossed myself in shaping this book.*

*My parents, Paul Jose and Annice Paul, have been my constant support throughout my life, in each and every endeavor of mine, and I also dedicate this book to them.*

# Table of Contents

About the Author ........ xi

About the Technical Reviewer ........ xiii

Acknowledgments ........ xv

Introduction ........ xvii

Chapter 1: Introduction to Serverless Technology ........ 1
- What Is Serverless? ........ 2
- Self-Managed vs. Fully Managed vs. Serverless Services ........ 2
  - Self-Managed Services ........ 2
  - Fully Managed Services ........ 3
  - Serverless Services on AWS ........ 4
- Why Serverless? ........ 9
- Serverless-First Mindset ........ 9
- A Bit About FaaS ........ 10
- Conclusion ........ 11

Chapter 2: Distributed Serverless Architectures ........ 13
- Key Characteristics of Distributed Systems ........ 13
  - Near-Zero Latency ........ 14
  - Fault Tolerant ........ 15
  - Highly Available ........ 16
  - Scalability ........ 16
  - Immutable Architecture ........ 16
- The Cloud and Distributed Systems ........ 16

Making a Solution Distributed ... 17
Orchestrating Actions ... 17
Collecting Data from Different Regions ... 18
Pros and Cons of Global Distributed Apps ... 19
Common Architectural Patterns ... 19
Event-Driven Architectures ... 19
Disaster Recovery Architectures ... 20
Conclusion ... 22
**Chapter 3: Event-Driven Architectures ... 23**
What Are Event-Driven Architectures? ... 23
Event Producer ... 24
Event Trigger ... 24
Event Processor ... 25
Event Consumer ... 26
Common Serverless Web Application Architecture ... 27
Adding Resiliency to the Serverless Web Application Architecture ... 31
Design a Serverless Streaming Event Processor ... 34
Designing a Serverless Email Service with Bounced Email Handling ... 38
Event-Driven Alerting Using Serverless ... 45
Conclusion ... 48
**Chapter 4: Disaster Recovery Architectures ... 49**
Introduction to Disaster Recovery Strategies ... 49
Disaster Recovery Strategies Based on Region ... 49
Geographic Topology of the AWS Cloud ... 50
Multi-AZ Disaster Recovery Strategy ... 52
Cross-Region Disaster Recovery Strategy ... 58
Serverless Database Disaster Recovery Implementation ... 67

Disaster Recovery Strategy Based on RTO and RPO ........ 71

Active Backups Only ........ 72

Active-Active Configuration ........ 73

Active-Passive Configuration ........ 73

Conclusion ........ 73

**Chapter 5: Serverless Data Platforms ........ 75**

Overview of Data Platforms ........ 75

Serverless Data Platform on AWS ........ 77

Data Ingestion Services ........ 78

Data Storage Services ........ 80

Data Consumption and Visualization Services ........ 84

Building a Serverless Data Analytics Application ........ 87

Implementing AWS Data Pipeline Service ........ 88

Conclusion ........ 93

**Chapter 6: Containers on Serverless ........ 95**

Overview of Containers ........ 95

Serverless Container Services on AWS ........ 96

Container Orchestration Services ........ 97

Container Hosting Services ........ 98

Container Registry Service ........ 98

Container Modernization ........ 99

Serverless Web Application Architecture Using Fargate ........ 99

Running Containers using Serverless Services on AWS ........ 103

Running Containers on Fargate ........ 103

Running Containers on Lambda ........ 111

Conclusion ........ 114

**Chapter 7: Multicloud Architectures.................................................. 115**

Types of Cloud Architectures.................................................. 115

Single-Cloud Architecture.................................................. 115

Hybrid Cloud Architecture.................................................. 116

Cloud-Agnostic Architecture.................................................. 119

Multicloud Architecture.................................................. 122

Distributed Cloud Architecture.................................................. 123

Polycloud Architecture.................................................. 127

Comparison of Cloud Architectures.................................................. 129

Conclusion.................................................. 130

**Chapter 8: Serverless Through the AWS Well-Architected Framework.............. 131**

Operational Excellence Pillar.................................................. 131

Perform Operations As Code.................................................. 132

Make Frequent, Small, Reversible Changes.................................................. 132

Refine Operations Procedures Frequently.................................................. 133

Anticipate Failure.................................................. 133

Learn from All Operational Failures.................................................. 133

Security Pillar.................................................. 134

Implement a Strong Identity Foundation.................................................. 134

Enable Traceability.................................................. 135

Automate Security Best Practices.................................................. 135

Protect Data in Transit and at Rest.................................................. 135

Keep People Away from Data.................................................. 136

Prepare for Security Events.................................................. 136

Reliability Pillar.................................................. 136

Automatically Recover from Failure.................................................. 136

Test Recovery Procedures.................................................. 137

Scale Horizontally to Increase Aggregate Workload Availability.................................................. 137

Stop Guessing Capacity.................................................. 137

Manage Change in Automation.................................................. 137

Performance Efficiency Pillar ........ 137
Democratize Advanced Technologies ........ 137
Go Global in Minutes ........ 138
Use Serverless Architectures ........ 138
Experiment More Often ........ 139
Consider Mechanical Sympathy ........ 139
Cost Optimization Pillar ........ 139
Implement Cloud Financial Management ........ 139
Adopt a Consumption Model ........ 139
Measure Overall Efficiency ........ 140
Stop Spending Money on Undifferentiated Heavy Lifting ........ 140
Analyze and Attribute Expenditure ........ 140
Sustainability Pillar ........ 140
Conclusion ........ 141
**Chapter 9: Looking Ahead ........ 143**
A Constantly Evolving Landscape ........ 143
The Co-existence of Serverless Architectures ........ 143
Serverless Without Lambda ........ 144
Driving the Growth Mindset ........ 144
Conclusion ........ 145
**Index ........ 147**

# About the Author

**Jithin Jude Paul** is a cloud architect and serverless advocate who is passionate about AWS technologies. In his decade-long career, he has been a software developer, full-stack engineer, cloud developer, DevOps engineer, cloud architect, and solution architect. He is currently working as an AWS solution architect and helps onboard customers to AWS.

Jithin was born in Kochi, Kerala. He graduated from Mahatma Gandhi University with a major in electronics and communication engineering. He enjoys engaging at meetups and workshops. He was a speaker at the AWS re: Invent conference, where he showcased the power of utilizing serverless components while architecting distributed systems. In his spare time, he enjoys playing the guitar, cooking, and spending time with his family.

# About the Technical Reviewer

**Akash Tyagi** has spent 13 years architecting, building, and testing software. He is an active member of the AWS Community Builder program and loves to write on various technical topics including DevOps, architecture, pipelines, and testing.

Akash holds an MTech degree from National University of Singapore (NUS) and is currently working in a fintech company in Singapore. He can be reached at `www.linkedin.com/in/akashdktyagi/`.

# Acknowledgments

I would like to thank Almighty God for giving me the wisdom, knowledge, and strength to complete this book. There were many personal hurdles while managing my family and writing this book, and our good Lord helped me to navigate through them to complete this book.

I would also like to thank the acquisitions editor of my book, Celestin Suresh John, as whenever I asked for an extension or had a query, he would patiently listen and offer a resolution. Also, I would like to thank the editor of my book, Jim Markham and Mark Powers, who reviewed my book and suggested changes wherever required. Thank you for your patience and input, Jim, Mark and Celestin; it has really helped me grow as an author.

Last but in no means least, I would like to thank my high school computer teacher, Professor C.V. Nagaraj, who not only taught me computer science but also ignited in me a profound interest in the world of programming and computers.

# Introduction

Cloud adoption is increasing on a daily basis, and serverless services on the cloud are increasing in number as well. Hence, it is important for all IT professionals to understand what *serverless* means and how serverless services are beneficial while designing applications. If you have no experience with serverless technologies, this book will serve as a good starting point, as I offer a detailed overview of the what, why, and how of serverless so that you understand its underlying concepts and related terms before moving on to serverless architectures.

As it is essential to design systems in a distributed manner nowadays, throughout this book I use distributed architectures and serverless components on AWS. Although I have used AWS services to implement the architectures, you can replace them with analogous services in Google Cloud, Azure, or any public cloud provider with minimal configuration changes, and the results will be more or less the same. That's the beauty of the cloud and of serverless. I hope this book helps you in your journey as a cloud enthusiast to build robust systems using serverless services.

You can find the source code used in this book at `https://github.com/apress/distributed-serverless-architecture-aws`.

If you have any suggestions or queries regarding this book, please reach out to me.

- *Email*: `jithinjudepaule@gmail.com`
- *LinkedIn*: `https://www.linkedin.com/in/jithinjudepaul/`

I hope you enjoy reading this book. May God bless you.

# CHAPTER 1

# Introduction to Serverless Technology

If you have been working in the software industry for any amount of time, you will have come across the term *serverless* in relation to many architectural decisions. So, what is serverless, and why write a book on serverless architectures exclusively?

Well, the answer to this question lies in the fact that serverless has grown from being a function as a service (FaaS) to a large landscape of exclusive serverless components. Serverless patterns are ubiquitous, and there are lots of typical architectures that follow the serverless track. Having spent years working in the serverless world, I will summarize a few patterns in this book that are commonly used while designing systems using AWS. But before that, let's understand what serverless is and what its key components are.

This chapter covers the following aspects:

- What serverless is
- Managed versus serverless services
- Serverless services on AWS
- Why you might want to go serverless
- Reference architecture for a serverless web application




J. J. Paul, *Distributed Serverless Architectures on AWS*, https://doi.org/10.1007/978-1-4842-9159-7_1

# What Is Serverless?

If you are like me, you might find the term *serverless* confounding the first time you hear it. After all, don't all web applications need to be hosted somewhere? Well, *serverless* doesn't mean that no servers are involved but that there are fewer servers to manage; rather, the way to go about this pattern is to leave server management to the cloud provider you are working with. In essence, you manage only the code that you work on, and the management of hosting, scaling, etc., is done by the cloud provider.

Before we dive deeper into serverless, let's understand the different types of services available in the cloud based on the level of management.

# Self-Managed vs. Fully Managed vs. Serverless Services

When it comes to different kinds of services in the cloud based on management overhead and level of control, we can divide them broadly into three categories: self-managed services, fully managed services, serverless services.

## Self-Managed Services

With self-managed services, the cloud provider shares a small amount of responsibility over the launched services. The developer has to take care of the configuration, scaling, security, patching, etc., for the application. Here the developer or the admin has maximum control over the application and can implement any desired configuration. We can also call this category of services *user-managed services.*

Self-managed services are mostly used either during a migration from on-premise to the cloud or when the application that is being developed needs to be highly configurable and controllable. Usually virtual machines are used to launch self-managed services.

For example, say we have configured a highly scalable Apache Kafka cluster and we are using it on our premises and decide to use the same configuration on the AWS cloud over the other queuing solutions. At this juncture, we can launch an EC2 instance and deploy the Kafka cluster inside the EC2 virtual machine. Figure 1-1 shows this implementation.

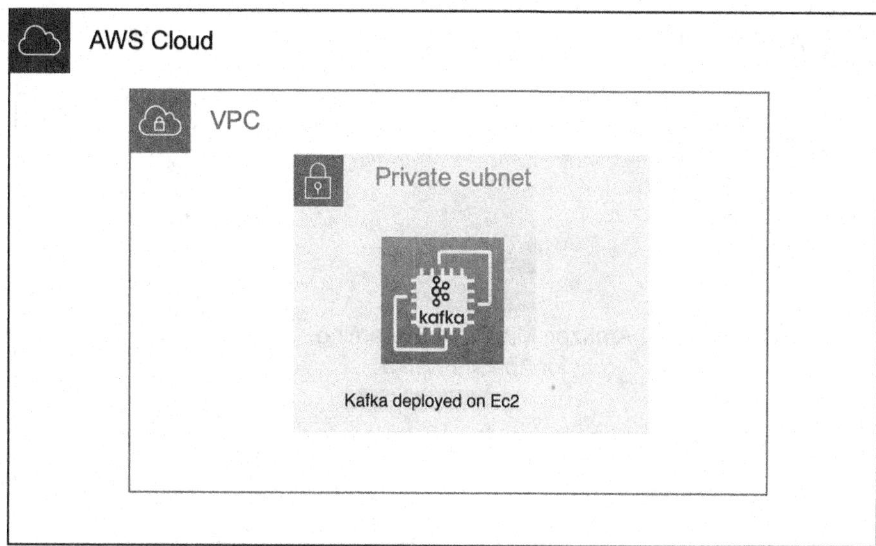


***Figure 1-1.*** *An example of a self-managed service*

## Fully Managed Services

In a fully managed service, the application developer just needs to choose the required configurations from the options available, and the service can be easily set up. The developer does not need to worry about the underlying hardware or its patching, availability, etc., as that is the responsibility of the cloud provider.

Some of the main reasons for choosing managed services are the ease of setup, less management overhead, and high availability. Let's consider the previous example of migrating an on-premise Kafka cluster to the cloud. If the team does not have the expertise to set up a Kafka cluster by themselves or they want less management overhead, the same Kafka cluster can be launched using the AWS Managed Streaming for Apache Kafka service, which is a fully managed, highly available Apache Kafka service. Figure 1-2 illustrates this.

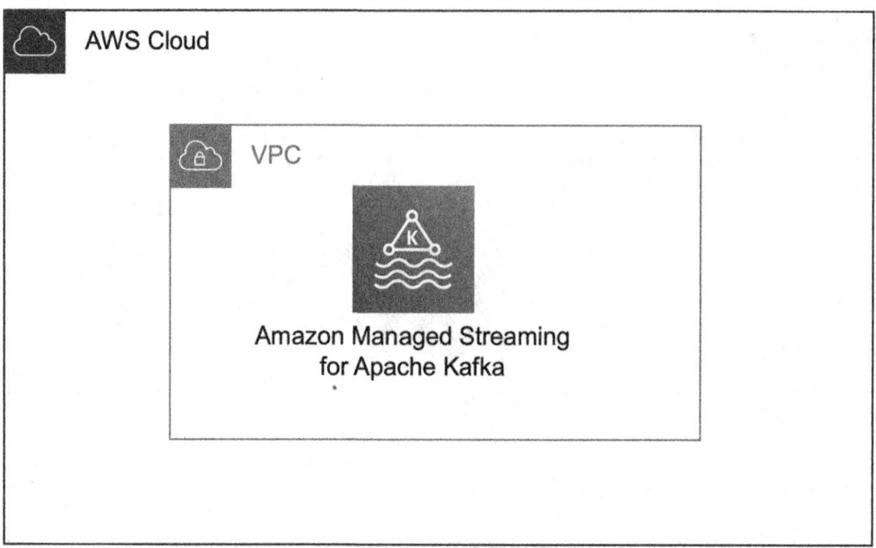


*Figure 1-2. An example of the AWS Managed Streaming for Apache Kafka service*

## Serverless Services on AWS

A serverless service is an abstracted, fully managed service where you only need to care about the function you are executing using the desired service. Unlike with fully managed services, you need to pay only for the time/requests for which you have used the service. That is, serverless follows a pay-per-use model.

Serverless services come in handy when you want to increase agility, optimize costs, and reduce infrastructure provisioning tasks. Let's consider the same example of a queuing system. If we need to replace the on-premise queuing system with a serverless one, we need to use Amazon's Simple Queue Service (SQS), which is a fully managed queuing service that eliminates the complexity associated with operating message-oriented architecture and reduces management overhead.

SQS can dynamically scale on demand with no limit to the number of messages per queue. It is also priced based on the number of requests per month, which includes a free tier of 1 million requests, making it significantly cheaper than the always-on messaging architectures. See Figure 1-3.

***Figure 1-3.*** *Amazon SQS, a serverless service from AWS*

Now let's look at some of the AWS serverless offerings in the areas of compute, application integration, and data storage; see Figure 1-4. Kindly note that the list of services from AWS gets updated frequently, and the following is accurate while I am writing this book. The latest list with all the AWS services is available at `https://aws.amazon.com`.

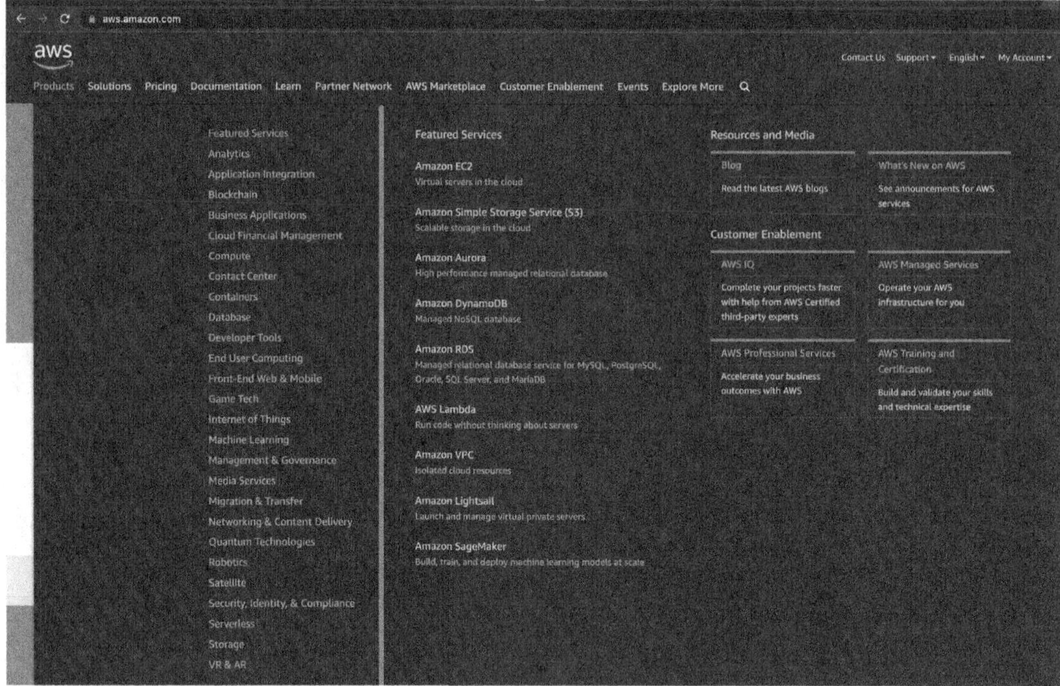


***Figure 1-4.*** *List of AWS services from the AWS documentation*

## Compute

Let's discuss the serverless services that AWS provides for compute.

- *AWS Lambda* is the FaaS offering from AWS with a pay-per-use pricing model. The user needs to focus only on the code that is being written, and AWS manages the underlying architecture. You will be seeing AWS Lambda being used in lots of architectures throughout this book as Lambda integrates with most AWS services.
- *The Fargate service* is a serverless compute service for containers; it works in conjunction with AWS EKS and ECS and provides the necessary compute required for the containers.

## Application Integration

AWS provides lots of serverless services for application integration ranging from messaging services to queuing services to event bus services, etc. Let's discuss them here:

- *Amazon Event Bridge* is the AWS serverless event bus offering used to build event-driven systems at scale.
- *AWS Step Functions* enables you to orchestrate your entire workflow by providing you with a visual workflow orchestrator.
- *Amazon SQS* is the serverless queuing system from AWS that helps you decouple systems and process them asynchronously.
- *Amazon SNS* is the fully managed messaging service from AWS that enables you to send messages between applications as well as to external communication devices.
- *The Amazon API Gateway* enables you to create, publish, and manage websocket and REST APIs on a variable or fixed scale.
- *AWS AppSync* is a fully managed service to develop GraphQL APIs as AppSync helps in managing the scaling and connections of GraphQL APIs.

## Data Store

AWS provides serverless services for relational databases, for nonrelational databases, and for object storage. Let's discuss them here:

- *Amazon S3* is a simple object storage service from AWS with very high availability and resiliency.
- *Amazon DynamoDb* is a key-value serverless data store with very high throughput and single-digit millisecond performance.
- *Amazon RDS Proxy* is the proxy service offered for Amazon's relational database services to make them more secure and scalable.
- *Amazon Aurora Serverless* is a MySQL- and Postgres-compatible relational database service from AWS. The serverless configuration of Aurora can autoscale on demand.

Figure 1-5 compares levels of abstraction in various tech stacks versus the amount of focus that can be attributed to application development.

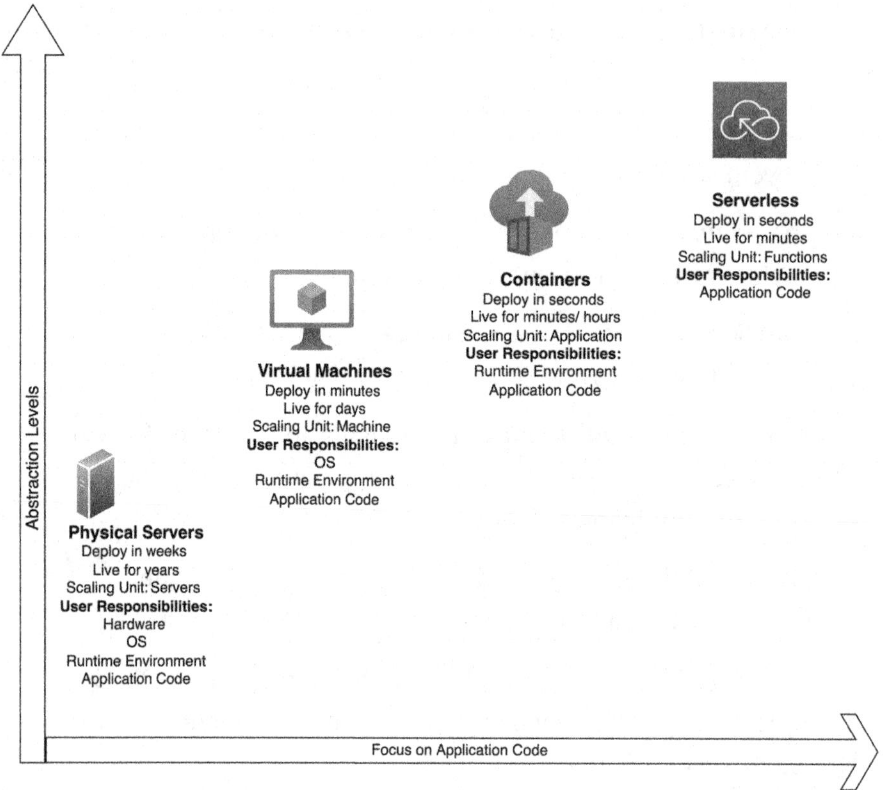


***Figure 1-5.*** *Abstraction levels versus application code focus in tech stacks*

So, in essence, serverless does the following:

- Shifts operational overhead to the cloud provider
- Provides servers that are managed by the cloud provider
- Provides fully managed scaling
- Provides near-zero downtime
- Provides very high availability

# Why Serverless?

More and more companies are adopting serverless architectures as part of their application development. The following are a few of the advantages of serverless services:

- *Saves money*: Because serverless services follow a pay-per-use model, you pay only for the time for which you use serverless components. This makes the entire architecture cost-effective.
- *Supports a green cloud*: As there is no dedicated hardware for the applications we develop, the resources that are being used for components are reusable. Also, the compute resources are allocated only when they are invoked and hence reduce the carbon footprint.
- *Offers high availability*: The serverless components are designed for high availability and near-zero fault tolerance as they are fully managed by cloud providers.
- *Has less infrastructure to manage*: As serverless services are managed by the respective cloud providers, we do not need to manage the infrastructure provisioning and management required for these services.

# Serverless-First Mindset

A serverless-first mindset is all about considering the serverless approach before any other approach and considering other approaches only if the serverless approach fails to meet the requirements (which rarely occurs). Hence, many projects that are migrated to the cloud initially start with a few serverless components and then integrate other systems as well in a phased manner.

Figure 1-6 shows a typical serverless pattern for a web application.

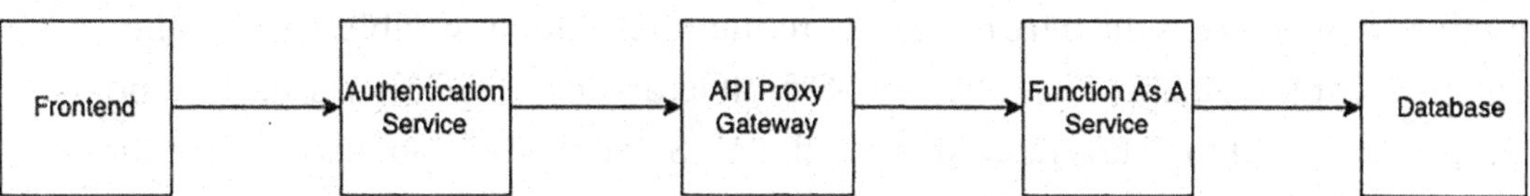


***Figure 1-6.*** *A typical serverless pattern*

All the components can be built using managed services from various cloud providers such as AWS, Azure, GCP, etc. All these features are managed by the cloud providers, including their availability, performance, and scaling.

# A Bit About FaaS

As shown in Figure 1-6, the FaaS component sits at the core of this architecture. We use a FaaS to write and host our code. Examples of functions as a service are Lambda from AWS, Azure Functions from Azure, and Cloud Functions from Google. One of the main reasons for the popularity of serverless design is the ease with which one can spin up a FAAS component and tear it down if not in use.

Lambda is the most common serverless compute service from AWS, and it can be triggered from most of the AWS services and is widely used in many serverless architectures.

Let's consider the scenario of a typical web application whose components have been replaced with their corresponding AWS components; see Figure 1-7.

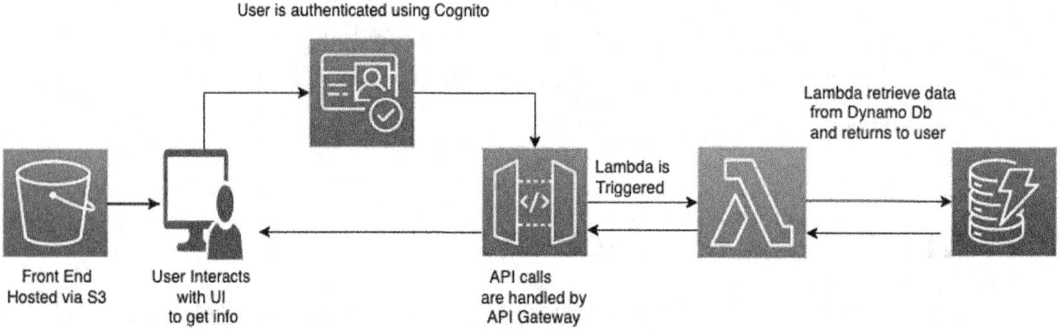


***Figure 1-7.*** *A serverless app modeled using AWS components*

This architecture contains the components required to set up a simple web application using serverless components alone. We can always extend this architecture and include components for content delivery, logging, monitoring, etc., but this architecture is the bare minimum requirements for a scalable, secure, and highly available web app. I have used this architecture in many projects, and all the components meet the SLAs mentioned in the AWS documentation. Let's look at these components at a high level:

- *Front end*: Though AWS S3 is categorized as a serverless data store, we can use it to host static websites as well.
- *Authentication*: We can use AWS Cognito as a highly scalable and secure solution for authentication, authorization, and user management. It supports sign-in with social identity providers, such as Apple, Facebook, Google, and Amazon, and with enterprise identity providers via SAML 2.0 and OpenID Connect.
- *API management*: API Gateway is a fully managed service. It's easy for developers to create, publish, maintain, monitor, and secure the RESTful and WebSocket APIs at any scale.
- *Lambda*: We can use Lambda to host RESTful APIs, and since it uses a cost-per-use model, it can save you money and offer scalability, resiliency, and high availability. I would say that serverless architectures started evolving when Lambda was released.
- *DynamoDB*: In this architecture, I have used DynamoDB as a NoSQL database. But if your web app requires a relational database service, you can use Aurora Serverless, which is built on top of MySQL or PostgreSQL.

# Conclusion

In this chapter, you learned what serverless is, what its advantages are, and you compared managed services to serverless services on AWS.

Over the next few chapters, you will see more complex architectures using all or some of the previously mentioned components of a serverless web application, as they are the building blocks of most serverless architectures.

CHAPTER 2

# Distributed Serverless Architectures

Any system that distributes its tasks across multiple components on the same network can be classified as a *distributed system*.

While there are multiple ways in which we can implement distributed systems, this chapter focuses on using serverless technology to build distributed architectures.

In this chapter, we'll look at some of the key characteristics of distributed architectures, their advantages and disadvantages, how to create a distributed solution using serverless, example architectures, and finally event-driven and disaster recovery architectures.

## Key Characteristics of Distributed Systems

The Internet that we use on a day-to-day basis can be categorized as a distributed system or, rather, a globally distributed system. Figure 2-1 shows a simple diagram of a distributed system.




J. J. Paul, *Distributed Serverless Architectures on AWS*, https://doi.org/10.1007/978-1-4842-9159-7_2

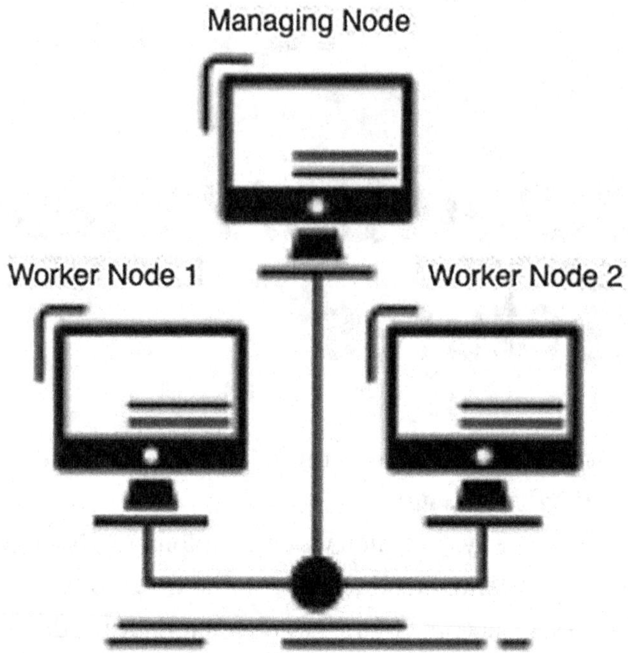


***Figure 2-1.*** *Distributed system*

Here the task to be executed is spread across multiple worker nodes, and it is managed centrally by a managing node; in short, the tasks are *distributed.* Most of the architectures we deal with in this book are distributed, so it is essential to understand a bit about this type of system. The following sections highlight some of the important characteristics of distributed systems.

## Near-Zero Latency

If we are building a distributed system, the dependent components in the system must have zero or minimum latency. This will ensure that the application that is running does not time out while waiting for various components to respond. This may not be achievable at all times, so we use a queuing mechanism to ensure that all the application cycles reach completion and there are no unprocessed stages in the application lifetime. Figure 2-2 provides a simple example of a distributed system using serverless where we are using Amazon SQS as a buffer for unprocessed images.

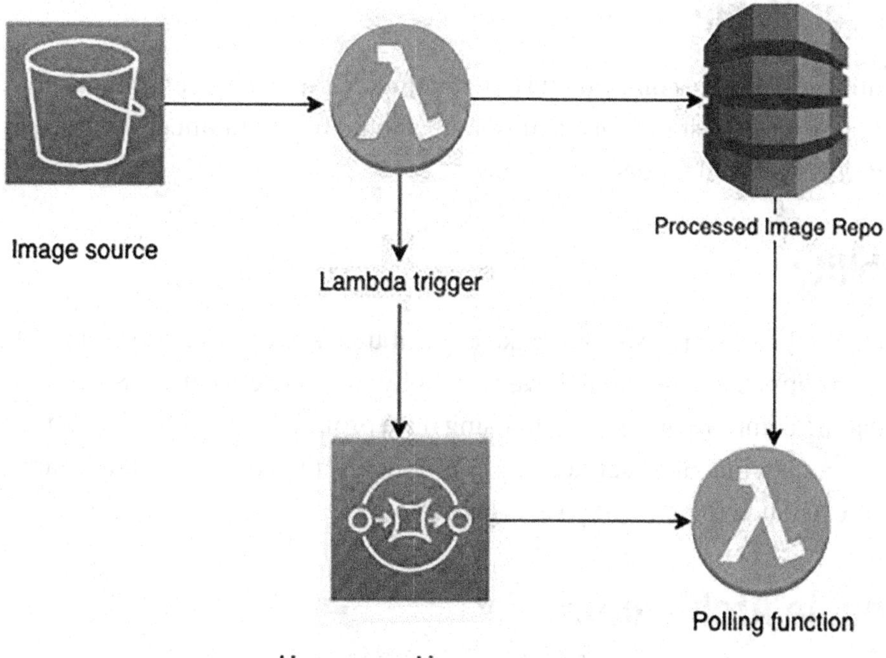


***Figure 2-2.*** *Using SQS as a buffer in a distributed system*

When an image is loaded to the S3 bucket, a Lambda trigger processes the image and stores it in the RDS instance. If some images go unprocessed because of latency or some technical issue, those images are stored in Amazon SQS directly instead of in a database. A Lambda function will then poll this queue periodically to ensure that the unprocessed images are processed and fed into the database.

In this manner, any latency in processing images is addressed by buffering it and processing it concurrently. This ensures that no images are lost, and at the same time, they are processed at a faster rate overall.

## Fault Tolerant

All the components in a distributed system must be fault tolerant; that is, if a component encounters a failure, it must be able to start a new instance of itself, or the traffic should be routed to a replica set accordingly. This ensures that the system works flawlessly without any errors or latency. For example, if the database we are using goes down, provisions must be made using monitoring systems to raise alerts and route traffic to a replica of the database that is in sync with the primary database.

## Highly Available

It is essential that the key components of a distributed system are highly available. That is, more than a single instance of a component should be maintained to reduce the load on the main system and for data resiliency.

## Scalability

Depending on the scenario, we can make a distributed system scalable or fixed. But 90 percent of the applications tend to have scalability as a desired feature. So, we need to ensure that the components we are choosing have provisions to scale automatically; or, if a component is a managed service, the components need to have enough capacity/ memory provisioned to perform on a larger scale.

## Immutable Architecture

An immutable architecture is a paradigm in which the servers cannot be modified once they are deployed. If there needs to be a change on the server, it needs to be replaced. Most distributed systems are designed to be immutable. For instance, if a container in a distributed system goes down, a new container with the same configuration is immediately spun up. Immutable architecture is closely entwined with IAC (Infrastructure As Code) tools such as Terraform and AWS CloudFormation that help us in building immutable architectures. AWS Lambda, which is the AWS function as a service, is an example of immutable architecture. In distributed systems, it is difficult to make changes in isolation. Hence, it is advisable to keep most components of a distributed system immutable.

# The Cloud and Distributed Systems

With the advent of cloud computing, distributed architectures have become more and more common. In fact, it's difficult to find a system that is not distributed nowadays because of the growing demand for autoscaled high-performing systems. But that doesn't mean that all systems need to be distributed in nature. For instance, real-time processing systems work well when the components are not distributed and are confined to a single system, as this will reduce latency. Let's look at the use cases for making a system distributed.

# Making a Solution Distributed

To make a system distributed, it needs to orchestrate actions, and its data needs to be collected from different regions. Let's review that now.

## Orchestrating Actions

A batch job that gets executed periodically on a server may not be the best use case to make a distributed solution. However, if the same batch job's output is used as input to other systems (as shown in Figure 2-3), then the system becomes distributed in nature. We have used serverless services to perform the batch processing asynchronously.

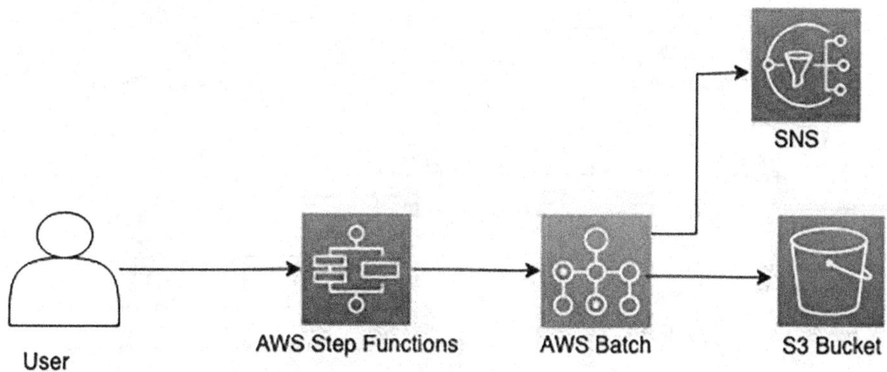


***Figure 2-3.*** *Distributed batch processing using serverless*

Here, the user initiates a step function, which in turn invokes the AWS batch job. The output of the batch job is stored in an S3 bucket, and at the same time, a notification is sent via SNS to a topic. All these services are independent of each other, making the solution distributed. Hence, any solution we are designing requires actions that need to be orchestrated, so it's better to make the solution distributed.

## Collecting Data from Different Regions

If we have a multi-region application and the data needs to be replicated in all regions, then it is imperative that we set up databases in all regions and keep updating the data to all databases in all regions so that the data is available to all the applications running in multiple regions. An alternative solution would be to design a globally distributed database like the Amazon Aurora global database, which can sync with all regions with minimum latency; the same database can be used by the central system in US East 1 to show metrics. Figure 2-4 shows four applications in four different regions. We are using the Aurora global database, and its master node is located in US East 1.

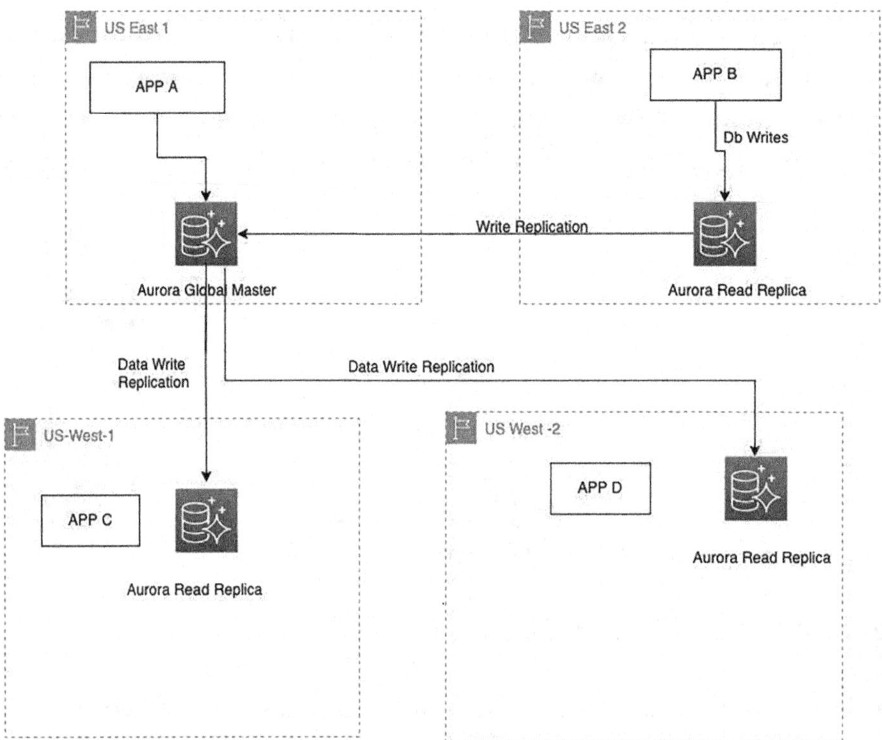


***Figure 2-4.*** *Aurora global database*

In the global database, we have one read and write instance located in the primary region (US East 1 here), and all other regions have read replicas. In Figure 2-4, APP B in the US East 2 region writes to the read replica of the Aurora global database, which then gets replicated to the primary region in US East 1 by using the write forwarding feature of Aurora. This replicated data is then further replicated to other read replicas in the US West 1 and US West 2 regions. Thus, having a globally distributed database helps us to sync all the databases with updated data seamlessly, as shown in the previous example.

## Pros and Cons of Global Distributed Apps

The following are some pros of globally distributed apps:

- Highly available
- Fault tolerant
- High performing
- Globally available and hence minimum latency to region-specific users

The following are some cons of global distributed apps:

- Monitoring in real-time is complex when compared with nondistributed systems because the observability metrics are collected from multiple resources and then aggregated.
- Complex design.
- High cost of implementation.

## Common Architectural Patterns

Now that we have an understanding of distributed systems, let me introduce you to a few architectural patterns we will be covering in this book from a high level.

### Event-Driven Architectures

The event-driven architecture is so far the most widely adopted serverless architecture pattern; in fact, events sit at the heart of any serverless application. Figure 2-5 provides an example of this type of architecture from a high level.

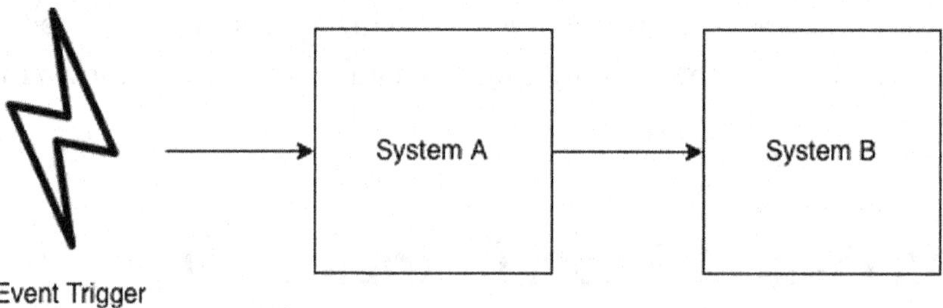


***Figure 2-5.*** *High-level event-driven system*

For event-driven architectures, the source is an event trigger, which triggers a system (System A in Figure 2-5), which further triggers other downstream systems. Few systems are entirely event-driven, whereas few systems use events as functionality in their application platform. We will be discussing this architecture in detail in Chapter 3.

## Disaster Recovery Architectures

There are different ways to configure your disaster recovery architectures. The disaster recovery (DR) strategy for a cloud provider mainly depends on three factors:

- The DR architecture needs to be within the same region or cross-region.
- The recovery time objective (RTO) is the minimum time required to restore a service.
- The recovery point objective (RPO) is the acceptable amount of loss incurred during recovery.

Figure 2-6 shows a typical DR architecture in an active-passive configuration. We will be discussing various types of DR architectures in Chapter 4 of this book.

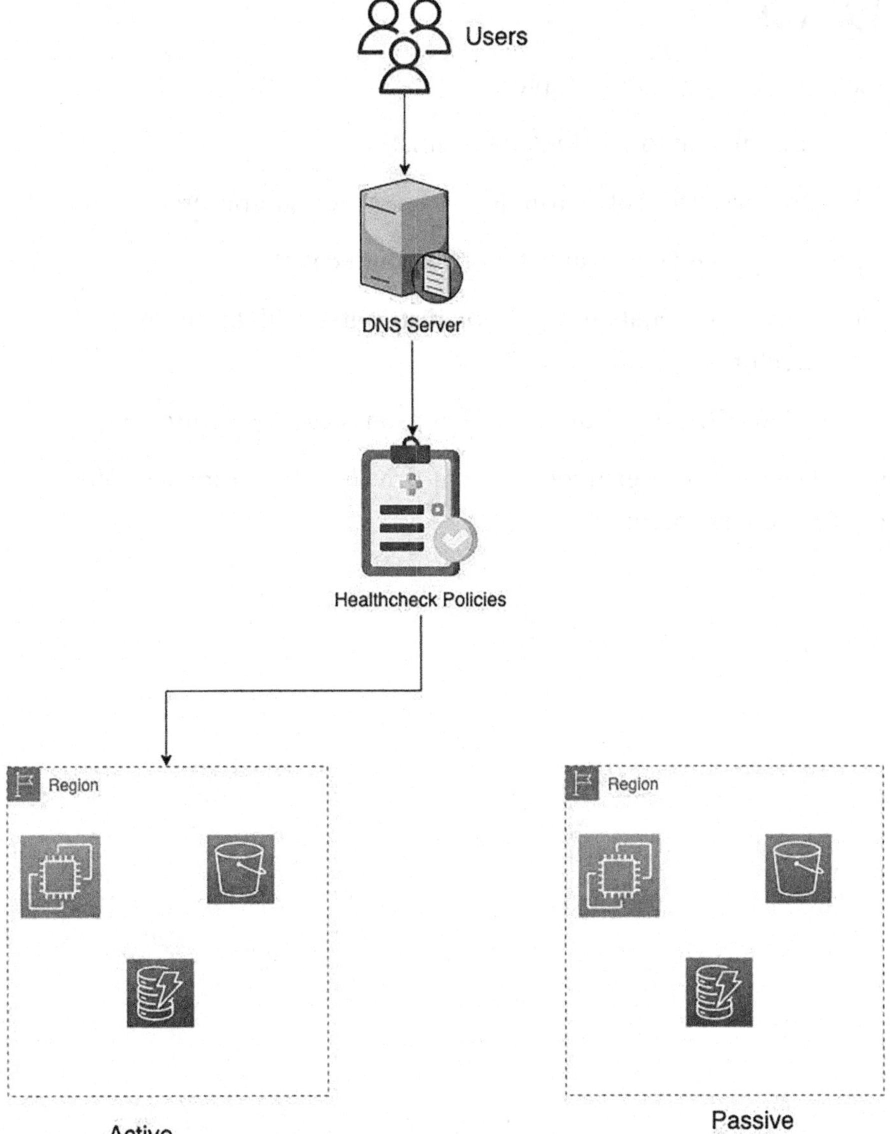


***Figure 2-6.*** *A typical DR architecture*

In this architecture, the DNS requests are resolved by running health checks using health check policies, and traffic is routed to a region only if it is healthy.

In addition to these architectures, there are numerous other architectural patterns for serverless systems. We will be discussing them in detail in the upcoming chapters.

# Conclusion

We covered the following in this chapter:

- An introduction to distributed systems
- Key characteristics of distributed systems with sample architectures
- Advantages and disadvantages of distributed systems
- How to arrive at making a solution distributed with example architectures
- Overview of the event-driven and disaster recovery architectures

In the next chapter, we'll explore the event-driven architecture using different categories of serverless components.

CHAPTER 3

# Event-Driven Architectures

In the previous chapters, you learned about serverless and distributed systems using AWS. Most of these systems included events in one form or another. Event-driven architectures, on the other hand, work based on the state changes or, rather, events. In this chapter, we'll cover the following:

- What event-driven architectures are
- Common event-driven architectures
- Different use cases for event-driven architectures

## What Are Event-Driven Architectures?

An *event* can be described as a change in state. For example, when a database goes down, it is a change from a stable state and hence can be categorized as an event.

Events make any system more responsive and robust. Let's discuss the anatomy of an event-driven architecture, which is visualized in Figure 3-1.

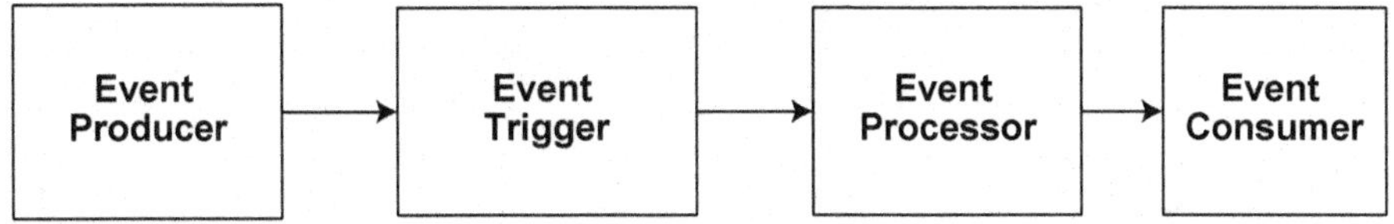


***Figure 3-1.*** *Anatomy of an event-driven architecture*

The general overview in Figure 3-1 can be used once or multiple times within a same application depending on the number of event producers and consumers. We'll go through each one in turn, beginning with event producers.




J. J. Paul, *Distributed Serverless Architectures on AWS*, https://doi.org/10.1007/978-1-4842-9159-7_3

# Event Producer

An *event producer* produces the necessary event to create a trigger. Generally, there would be an event source that produces events either at regular intervals or intermittently. Figure 3-2 shows a few examples of event producers.

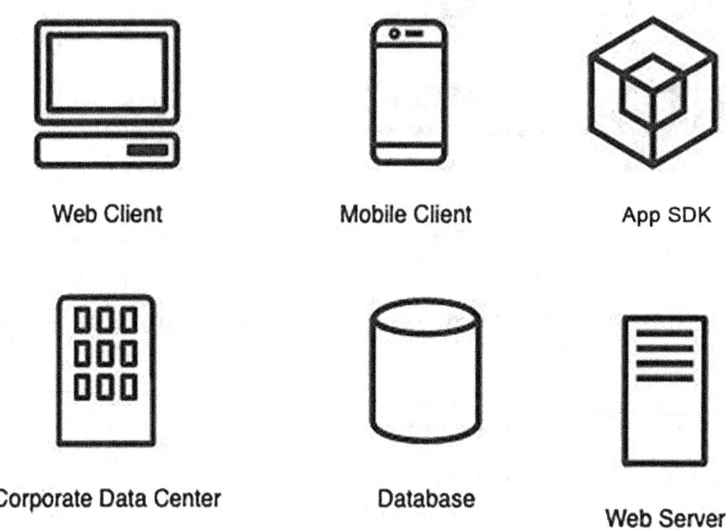


***Figure 3-2.*** *Examples of event producers*

# Event Trigger

An *event trigger* is a predefined action that needs to be executed when the expected event occurs. For example, if we keep an S3 trigger to execute a Lambda function when a Put event happens in a bucket, then the S3 trigger is the event trigger here, as illustrated in Figure 3-3.

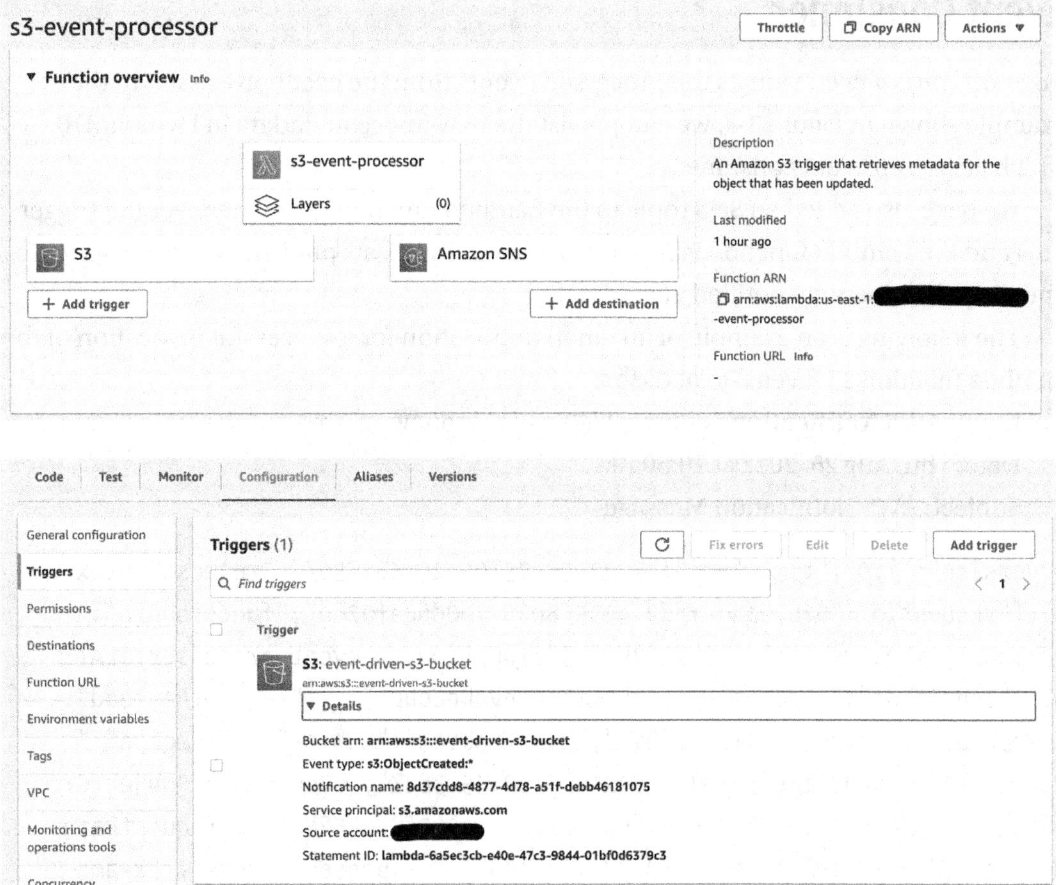


***Figure 3-3.** S3 event trigger for Lambda function*

Figure 3-3 shows the example of an S3 trigger, which invokes a Lambda function when an object is put in the S3 bucket `event-driven-s3-bucket`.

## Event Processor

An *event processor* processes the events that it receives from the event source. In the example in Figure 3-3, the Lambda function, `s3-event-processor`, processes the events from the S3 bucket.

## Event Consumer

An *event consumer* consumes the processed events from the event processor. In the example shown in Figure 3-3, we can persist the new image metadata in DynamoDB, which acts as an event consumer.

We have also added an SNS topic to the Lambda function, and whenever the trigger fires and the Lambda function is invoked successfully, it gets published to the SNS topic, and the subscribers get notified accordingly.

The following is an example of an email notification for a successful invocation of the Lambda function `s3-event-processor`:

From: **AWS Notifications** <no-reply@sns.amazonaws.com>

Date: Thu, Aug 25, 2022 at 10:50 AM

Subject: AWS Notification Message


```
{"version":"1.0","timestamp":"2022-08-25T05:20:46.750Z","requestContex
t":{"requestId":"6f679aad-fad9-4335-8d20-7d0d6cafa26e","functionArn":"
arn:aws:lambda:us-east-1:857312989998:function:s3-event-processor:$LATE
ST","condition":"Success","approximateInvokeCount":1},"requestPayload":
{"Records":[{"eventVersion":"2.1","eventSource":"aws:s3","awsRegion":"
us-east-1","eventTime":"2022-08-25T05:20:45.388Z","eventName":"ObjectCr
eated:Put","userIdentity":{"principalId":"A1L7AD0675FNBJ"},"requestPara
meters":{"sourceIPAddress":"49.37.162.140"},"responseElements":{"x-amz-
request-id":"YCJA250DTBJHWD5P","x-amz-id-2":"GWS5XrDa3XeNhkcqZfZW3bL5o/
watXxBDH2Dk/QWTMkl7GUmqoXbJCeutM43a+3EKxUCU56QDEBSE6qqoLw9g21WPLvxR7pi"},
"s3":{"s3SchemaVersion":"1.0","configurationId":"8d37cdd8-4877-4d78-a51f-
debb46181075","bucket":{"name":"event-driven-s3-bucket","ownerIdentity":
{"principalId":"A1L7AD0675FNBJ"},"arn":"arn:aws:s3:::event-driven-s3-bucket
"},"object":{"key":"Screenshot+2022-01-28+at+6.04.38+PM.png","size":713421,
"eTag":"88f1384ec940264cef069bd1581d60af","sequencer":"00630706AD44AF8D52"}
}}]},"responseContext":{"statusCode":200,"executedVersion":"$LATEST"},"resp
onsePayload":"image/png"}
```


Now, let's take a look at a few commonly used event-driven architectures.

## Common Serverless Web Application Architecture

In the example shown in Figure 3-4, we have a serverless web application that is hosted on AWS.

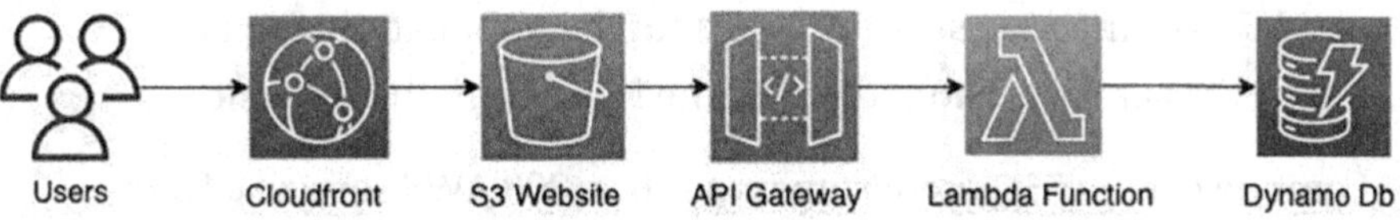


***Figure 3-4.*** *Common serverless web application architecture*

The following are its main components:

a) **CloudFront**

The CloudFront service is the content delivery service from AWS. It can be integrated with the S3 bucket used for static hosting and integrates with the AWS security tools such as AWS WAF, AWS Shield, etc. It ensures that the static content is served via multiple edge locations, decreasing latency and increasing performance.

b) **S3 Bucket**

Simple Storage Service is a fully managed object storage service from S3. The Static Website Hosting property of this service enables an S3 bucket to be used as a host to static content; or, rather, the front-end code as the S3 standard class has an availability and durability greater than 99 percent. It's a perfect fit for a front-end web application as it automatically scales under the hood when the request rate is high.

c) **API Gateway**

The API Gateway is a fully managed service from AWS that enables users to create, publish, maintain, monitor, and secure APIs at any scale. It can be used to create REST APIs as well as WebSocket APIs. Here we use API Gateway to trigger a Lambda function. The API calls are received from the front-end code hosted in S3, and upon reaching the API Gateway, the REST API endpoint request gets handed over to the Lambda function, which hosts the back-end APIs.

d) **Lambda**

AWS Lambda is a function-as-a-service offering from AWS, which enables you to host your application code, and the computing environment for it is fully managed by AWS without the need to provision or manage servers. Note that the application size and micro VMs are provisioned under the hood from the AWS side.

Lambda can be triggered from more than 200 AWS services. Here we are hosting our REST APIs in the Lambda function.

e) **DynamoDB**

Amazon DynamoDB is the NoSQL offering from Amazon that stores data as a key-value pair. DynamoDB supports high-traffic, extremely scaled events and can handle millions of queries per second. In our example, we are using DynamoDB to retrieve master data and persist transactional data.

The previous application can be provisioned through Terraform or any other infrastructure-as-a-code tool such as a serverless framework, AWS CDK, AWS CloudFormation, etc. I have used Terraform to provision the architecture in Figure 3-4. Note that I have excluded the CloudFront module from the Terraform provisioning as CloudFront constitutes a content delivery service that serves the front end of the serverless web application and is not part of the web application as such. I have included it in the architecture as it's a commonly used pattern. You can provision the environment by cloning this GitHub repo (`https://github.com/jithinjudepaule/Distributed_Serverless_Architectures_Book`).

Also, I have included a sample Hello World Lambda function for the Lambda function module. Feel free to replace it with your custom Lambda code.

---

It's beyond the scope of this book to explain the Terraform code line by line. I have included the relevant information in the GitHub repo mentioned earlier.

---

Once you apply any module, you will get the output shown in Figure 3-5. (I have applied the Lambda module here; the output will be similar for API Gateway, S3, and other modules.)

```
Jithins-MacBook-Pro backend-compute % terraform apply -var-file="lambda.tfvars"

Terraform used the selected providers to generate the following execution plan. Resource actions are indicated with the
following symbols:
  + create

Terraform will perform the following actions:

  # module.lambda.aws_iam_role.iam_for_lambda will be created
  + resource "aws_iam_role" "iam_for_lambda" {
      + arn                   = (known after apply)
      + assume_role_policy    = jsonencode(
            {
              + Statement = [
                  + {
                      + Action    = "sts:AssumeRole"
                      + Effect    = "Allow"
                      + Principal = {
                          + Service = "lambda.amazonaws.com"
                        }
                      + Sid       = ""
                    },
                ]
              + Version   = "2012-10-17"
            }
        )
      + create_date           = (known after apply)
      + force_detach_policies = false
      + id                    = (known after apply)
      + managed_policy_arns   = (known after apply)
      + max_session_duration  = 3600
      + name                  = "serverless-iam-role"
      + name_prefix           = (known after apply)
      + path                  = "/"
      + tags_all              = (known after apply)
      + unique_id             = (known after apply)

      + inline_policy {
          + name   = (known after apply)
          + policy = (known after apply)
        }
    }
```

***Figure 3-5.*** *Output of Terraform apply for the Lambda module*

```
  # module.lambda.aws_lambda_function.serverless will be created
  + resource "aws_lambda_function" "serverless" {
      + architectures                  = (known after apply)
      + arn                            = (known after apply)
      + filename                       = "lambda_function.zip"
      + function_name                  = "serverless-web-application"
      + handler                        = "lambda_function.lambda_handler"
      + id                             = (known after apply)
      + invoke_arn                     = (known after apply)
      + last_modified                  = (known after apply)
      + memory_size                    = 128
      + package_type                   = "Zip"
      + publish                        = false
      + qualified_arn                  = (known after apply)
      + reserved_concurrent_executions = -1
      + role                           = (known after apply)
      + runtime                        = "python3.9"
      + signing_job_arn                = (known after apply)
      + signing_profile_version_arn    = (known after apply)
      + source_code_hash               = (known after apply)
      + source_code_size               = (known after apply)
      + tags                           = {
          + "Application" = "serverless"
          + "terraform"   = "true"
        }
      + tags_all                       = {
          + "Application" = "serverless"
          + "terraform"   = "true"
        }
      + timeout                        = 90
      + version                        = (known after apply)

      + ephemeral_storage {
          + size = (known after apply)
        }

      + tracing_config {
          + mode = (known after apply)
        }
    }
```

***Figure 3-5.*** *(continued)*

```
Plan: 2 to add, 0 to change, 0 to destroy.

Do you want to perform these actions?
  Terraform will perform the actions described above.
  Only 'yes' will be accepted to approve.

  Enter a value: yes

module.lambda.aws_iam_role.iam_for_lambda: Creating...
module.lambda.aws_iam_role.iam_for_lambda: Creation complete after 3s [id=serverless-iam-role]
module.lambda.aws_lambda_function.serverless: Creating...
module.lambda.aws_lambda_function.serverless: Still creating... [10s elapsed]
module.lambda.aws_lambda_function.serverless: Creation complete after 15s [id=serverless-web-application]

Apply complete! Resources: 2 added, 0 changed, 0 destroyed.
```

***Figure 3-5.*** *(continued)*

Once the `apply` is complete, you will get the outputs that you have defined in the `Outputs` section of your code (I have included the Lambda ARN here).

```
Outputs:
lambda_arn = "arn:aws:lambda:us-east-1            :function:serverless-web-
application"
```

# Adding Resiliency to the Serverless Web Application Architecture

The web application introduced in Figure 3-4 would serve the purpose if the web traffic is relatively small. But if the traffic is very high and the customer does not want any API calls to be lost, then we should retry the Failed API calls. In Figure 3-6, we have made a provision for this resiliency feature.

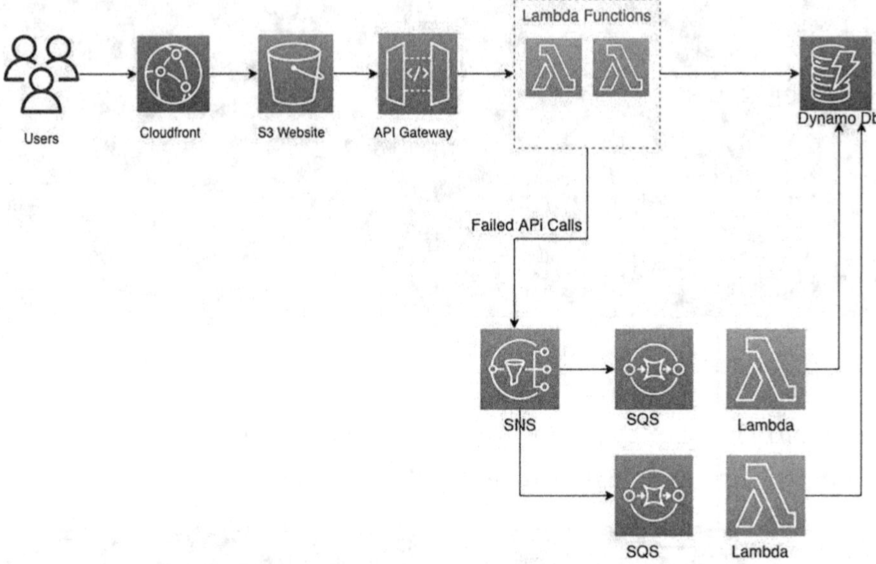


***Figure 3-6.*** *A highly resilient event-driven application*

Before we move on, let's first understand the components that will help us achieve this resiliency.

## Simple Notification Service

Amazon Simple Notification Service (Amazon SNS) is a fully managed messaging service in a Pub-Sub model. SNS enables its users to send notifications such as emails, messages, or posts directly to HTTP endpoints. It can send messages directly to an application (A2A) or to a person (A2P). In the previous example, the API calls to DynamoDB that did not succeed are passed to the SNS topic, which has different topics for different API calls. For example, if the previous system is an e-commerce web application, then the different topics can be Place Order API Topic, Payment Gateway API Topic, etc.

## Simple Queue Service

Amazon Simple Queue Service (SQS) is a fully managed message queuing service that enables you to scale elastically based on demand. The messages you can send through the standard queues are nearly unlimited, which makes it the ideal candidate for async processing.

In the example shown in Figure 3-6, we are using SNS to fan out the messages to the corresponding SQS queues, and these queues act as event sources for the corresponding Lambda functions. This subscriber Lambda further processes the failed API calls to be sent to DynamoDB for persistence.

We can add an SQS trigger to a Lambda function, as shown in Figure 3-7.

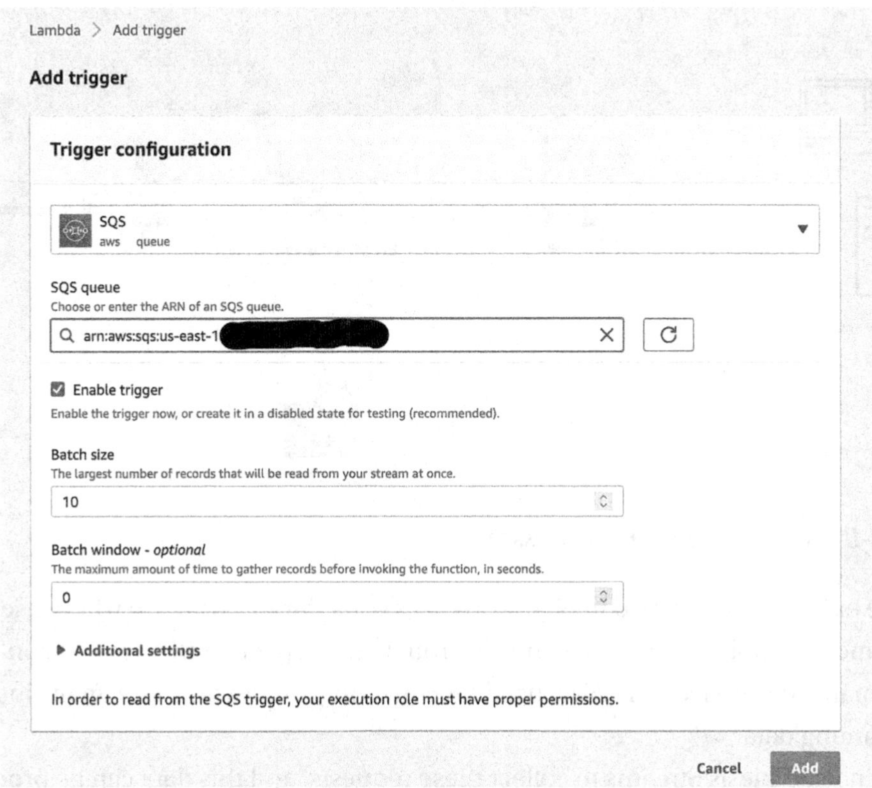


***Figure 3-7.*** *SQS trigger to Lambda function*

We need to configure the following Mandatory parameter for the SQS queue:

- **Batch size**: Here the Batch size is a parameter we need to configure. It indicates the number of records to send to the Lambda function in each batch.
- **Batch window**: This is an optional parameter, and it indicates the time window before invoking the function.

# Design a Serverless Streaming Event Processor

Nowadays, streaming data is in use everywhere. Whether streaming sports events, live conferences, etc., it is ubiquitous. So, architectures that handle streaming data are also becoming popular. Figure 3-8 shows a streaming event processor using event-driven architecture.

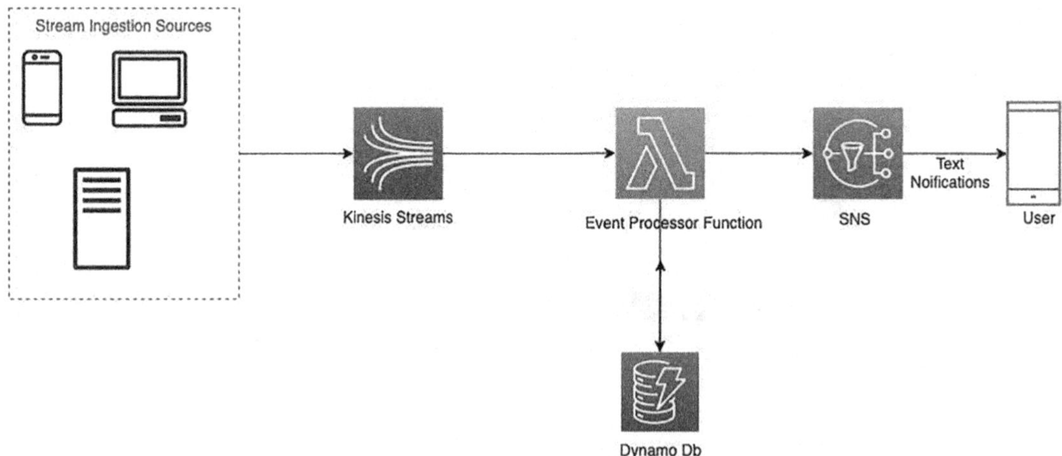


***Figure 3-8.*** *Streaming event processor*

In the example established in Figure 3-8, let's consider the scenario where users of web and mobile applications raise requests from their respective clients. Amazon Kinesis is a fully managed service from AWS used for collecting, processing, and analyzing real-time streaming data.

We can use Kinesis Streams to collect these requests, and this data can be processed in the event processor Lambda function that has kept Kinesis Streams as an event source. Whenever a record is ingested into the Kinesis stream, it invokes the Lambda function to process the record and notify the user using SNS on the status of the request. The request details can further be persisted in the DynamoDB table.

We can scale this solution from a few users to thousands of users as Amazon Kinesis can handle any amount of streaming data and process data from thousands of sources with very low latencies. And as the solution is serverless, we need to pay only for the processed records, and we do not need to allocate any preprovisioned capacity beforehand.

We can add Kinesis Streams as a trigger for the Lambda function as shown in Figure 3-9.

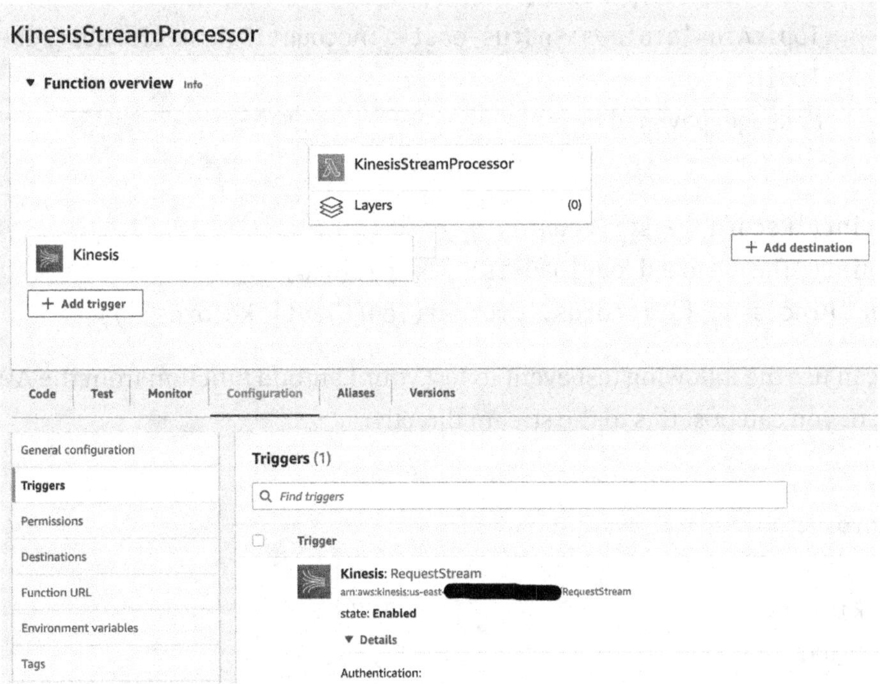

***Figure 3-9.** Adding Kinesis Streams*

The Kinesis records can be processed in the Lambda function using the following code written in Python using Boto3:

```
import base64
import json
import boto3
def lambda_handler(event, context):
  count=0
  client = boto3.client('sns')
  #Record processing starts
  for record in event['Records']:
      count=count+1
      # Kinesis data is base64 encoded so decode here
      payload = base64.b64decode(record['kinesis']['data']).decode('utf-8')
  #code to pass the payload and  call other AWS services here
```

```
#As per the above example, we can publish this payload to the SNS
topics here
    response = client.publish(
         TopicArn='arn:aws:sns:us-east-1:AccountID:KinesisSubscriber
         Topic',
         Message=payload
     )

    print('Record '+ str(count))
    print("The Decoded payload is: " + payload)
return 'Processed {} records.'.format(len(event['Records']))
```

You can use the following test event to test your Lambda function from the AWS Console, or you can post this to the stream directly:


```
{
   "Records": [
     {
       "kinesis": {
         "partitionKey": "partitionKey-03",
         "kinesisSchemaVersion": "1.0",
         "data": "SGVsbG8sIFRoaXMgaXMgYSB0ZXN0IG1lc3NhZ2UgZnJvbSB0aGUg
         S2luZXNpcyBzdHJlYW0u",
         "sequenceNumber": "49545115243490985018280067714973144582180062
         593244200961",
         "approximateArrivalTimestamp": 1428537600
       },
       "eventSource": "aws:kinesis",
       "eventID": "shardId-000000000000:495451152434909850182800677149
       73144582180062593244200961",
       "invokeIdentityArn": "arn:aws:iam::SAMPLE2",
       "eventVersion": "1.0",
       "eventName": "aws:kinesis:record",
       "eventSourceARN": "arn:aws:kinesis:SAMPLE2",
       "awsRegion": "us-east-1"
     },
```

```
      {
      "kinesis": {
        "partitionKey": "partitionKey-04",
        "kinesisSchemaVersion": "1.0",
        "data": "SGVsbG8sIFRoaXMgaXMgdGhlIHNlY29uZCB0ZXN0IG1lc3NhZ2UgZn
        JvbSB0aGUgS2luZXNpcyBzdHJlYW0u",
        "sequenceNumber": "49545115243490985018280067714973144582180062593244200961",
        "approximateArrivalTimestamp": 1428537600
      },
      "eventSource": "aws:kinesis",
      "eventID": "shardId-000000000000:49545115243490985018280067714
      973144582180062593244200961",
      "invokeIdentityArn": "arn:aws:iam::SAMPLE2",
      "eventVersion": "1.0",
      "eventName": "aws:kinesis:record",
      "eventSourceARN": "arn:aws:kinesis:SAMPLE2",
      "awsRegion": "us-east-1"
    }
  ]
}
```

You will get the output shown in Figure 3-10 from the Lambda console, which contains the details of the message as well as its status.

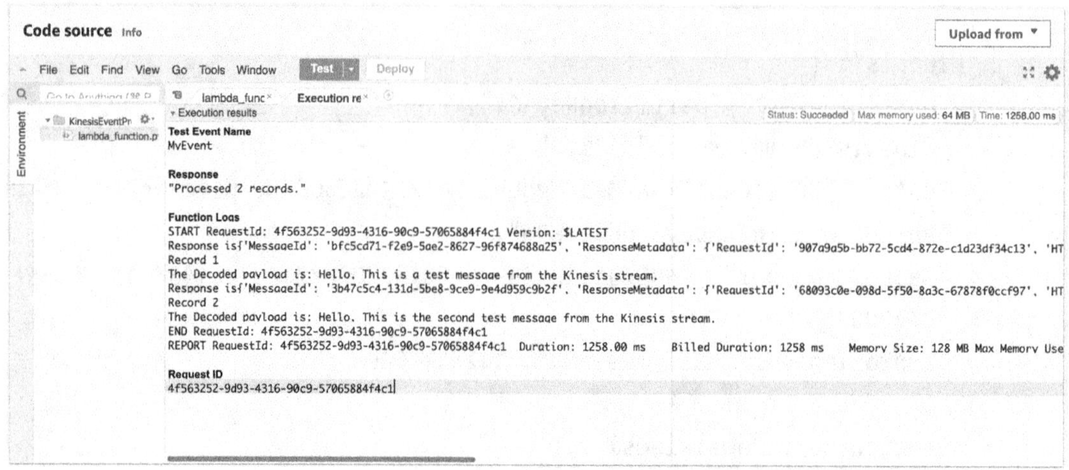

*Figure 3-10.* *Output of the Lambda test event*

As you would have observed, processing streaming events with serverless components is simple and cost effective. The solution mentioned in Figure 3-8 can be plugged into any architecture at any scale. That is the raw power of serverless services.

# Designing a Serverless Email Service with Bounced Email Handling

Figure 3-11 shows the emailing service that monitors and processes bounced emails. The architecture for the emailing service is simple; we have a Lambda function that processes the email request payload it receives and, using the AWS SDK, invokes the Amazon Simple Email Service, which is Amazon's emailing service, and sends the mail to the required mailbox.

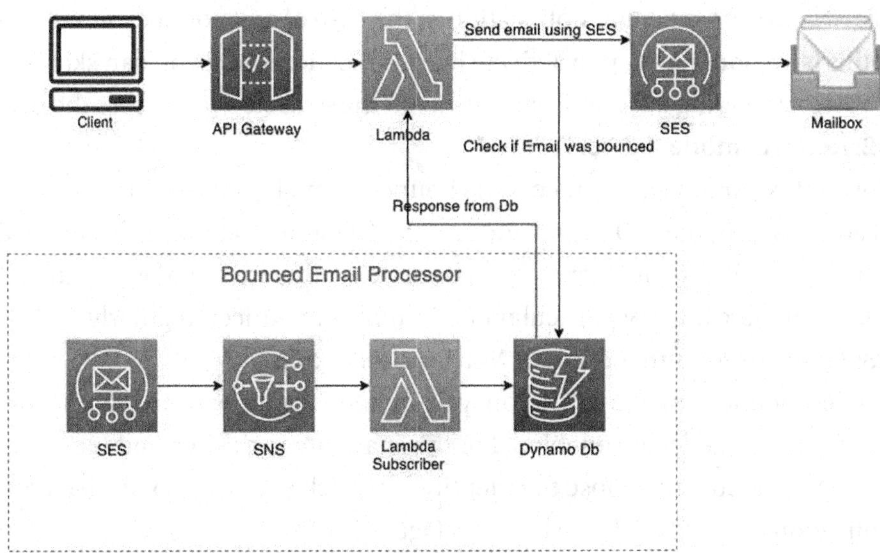


***Figure 3-11.*** *An email service that handles bounced emails as well*

So then, the obvious question is why do we need all the extra components and workflows there if an email can be sent using a simple API call? What is the need for handling bounced emails?

The answer to this question lies in the AWS service limits for emails. As per the AWS documentation, "The bounce rate for your account should remain below 5%. If the bounce rate for your account exceeds 10%, we might temporarily pause your account's ability to send email" (`https://docs.aws.amazon.com/pinpoint/latest/userguide/channels-email-deliverability-dashboard-bounce-complaint.html`).

So, we need to check whether the email address to which we are about to send mail was a bounced email or not. To do that, we need a list of bounced emails persisted in a persistent store that we can query before sending an email. The bounced email processor helps us to achieve that. Let's understand this in detail.

We need to perform the following steps to extract bounced emails and persist them in DynamoDB, which can later be queried against before sending an email.

**Step1: Create an SNS Topic for Receiving Bounced Emails.**

When the bounced email event occurs, we need to have a notification system in place that will send notifications. We can use the Amazon Simple Notification Service (SNS) for this. Create an SNS topic and if required add an email subscription to it. This will enable SNS to send an email notification in the case of any bounced email. (Kindly note that this is an optional step to activate live notifications, and you can skip it if required as we are adding a Lambda subscriber in the next step to process the event.)

**Step 2: Add a Lambda Subscriber to It.**

The job of this Lambda is to process the bounced email notification payload, extract the email address from the JSON, and add it to the DynamoDB table. If the email already exists in the DynamoDB table, increase its count by 1; otherwise, add a new item. By this, we get to know if there are any particular emails that get bounced regularly.

**Step 3: Enable the Bounced Email Notification in SES.**

To enable a bounce email notification, you should first choose the identity for which the bounced emails need to be enabled. For this, navigate to the Verified Identities option in the left menu and choose the identity for which you need to receive bounced email notifications for and click, as shown in Figure 3-12.

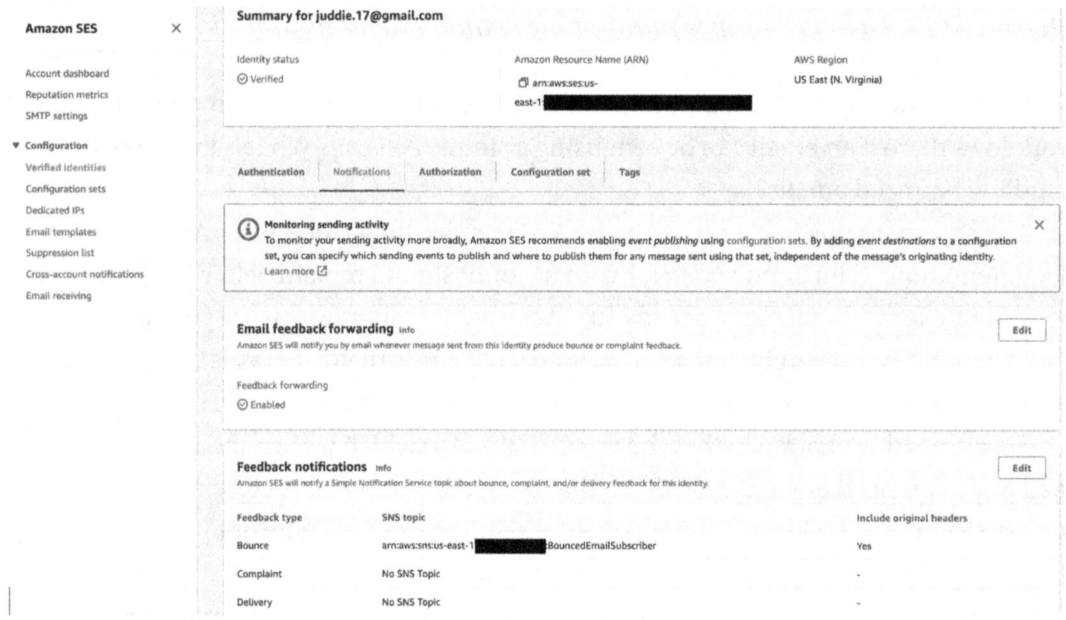


***Figure 3-12.*** *Enabling bounced email notification*

Now, in the event of a bounced email event, there should be a notification sent out. We created the SNS topic in step 1 for this purpose, and we can add it to the Bounce Feedback configuration. Go to the Notifications tab and edit the Feedback Notifications section by adding the SNS topic for bounced emails that you created in step 1, as illustrated in Figure 3-13.

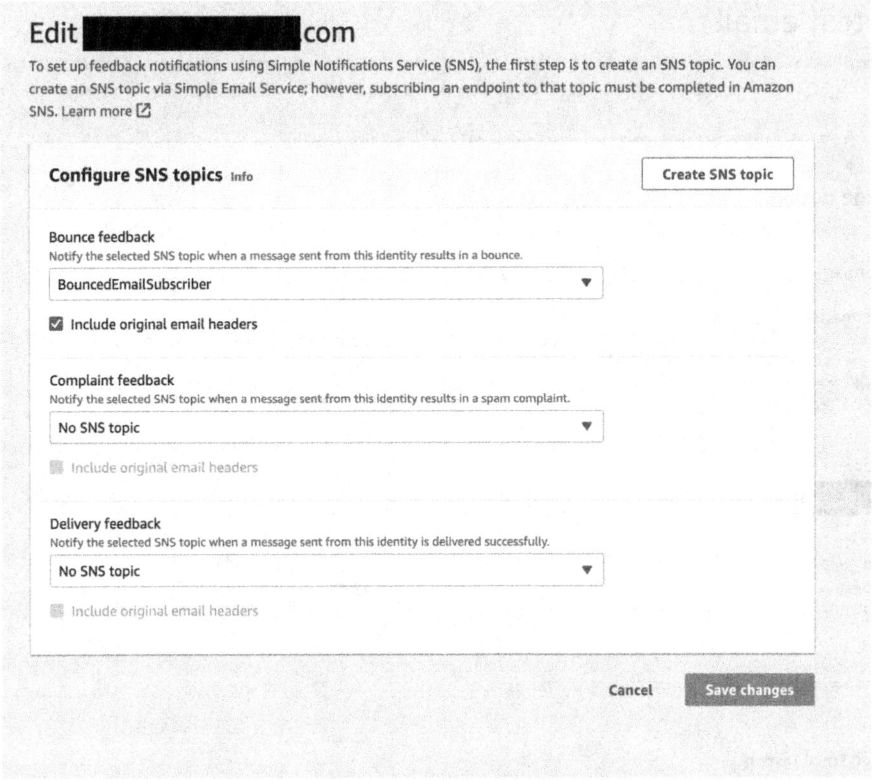

***Figure 3-13.*** *Adding the subscriber for bounced emails*

The previous steps ensure that all bounced emails are processed by the Lambda function, and from the Lambda function it can be persisted to DynamoDB or any other persistence store.

**Step 4: Test and verify the flow.**

AWS gives us the option to send test emails to check the bounced email processing flow, as shown in Figure 3-14.

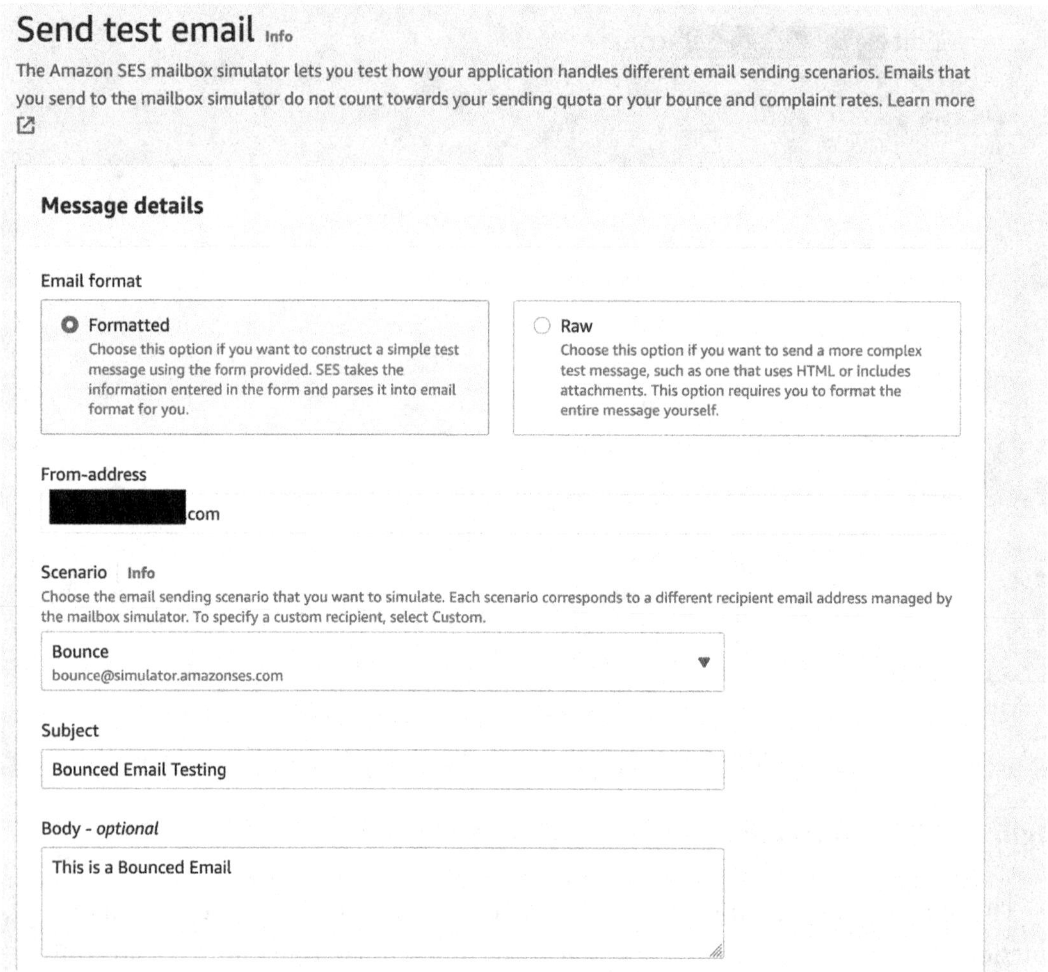

Send test email Info

The Amazon SES mailbox simulator lets you test how your application handles different email sending scenarios. Emails that you send to the mailbox simulator do not count towards your sending quota or your bounce and complaint rates. Learn more

Message details

Email format

Formatted
Choose this option if you want to construct a simple test message using the form provided. SES takes the information entered in the form and parses it into email format for you.

Raw
Choose this option if you want to send a more complex test message, such as one that uses HTML or includes attachments. This option requires you to format the entire message yourself.

From-address

.com

Scenario Info
Choose the email sending scenario that you want to simulate. Each scenario corresponds to a different recipient email address managed by the mailbox simulator. To specify a custom recipient, select Custom.

Bounce
bounce@simulator.amazonses.com

Subject

Bounced Email Testing

Body - *optional*

This is a Bounced Email

***Figure 3-14.** Setting up a test email*

If we check the CloudWatch logs for the bounced email subscriber Lambda function, we can see that it has logged a notification for a bounced email, as shown in Figure 3-15.

```
The Bounced Message:
{
    "notificationType": "Bounce",
    "bounce": {
        "feedbackId": "01000182f20f0ff7-9a454606-644e-41a6-b2c9-10f08b334983-000000",
        "bounceType": "Permanent",
        "bounceSubType": "General",
        "bouncedRecipients": [
            {
                "emailAddress": "bounce@simulator.amazonses.com",
                "action": "failed",
                "status": "5.1.1",
                "diagnosticCode": "smtp; 550 5.1.1 user unknown"
            }
        ],
        "timestamp": "2022-08-31T04:00:49.000Z",
        "remoteMtaIp": "34.201.181.44",
        "reportingMTA": "dns; a48-97.smtp-out.amazonses.com"
    },
    "mail": {
        "timestamp": "2022-08-31T04:00:49.220Z",
        "source": ████████.com",
        "sourceArn": "arn:aws:ses:us-east-1████████identity/juddie.17@gmail.com",
        "sourceIp": "49.37.162.140",
        "callerIdentity": "root",
        "sendingAccountId": ████████
        "messageId": "01000182f20f0e44-7bd6d91b-e248-45c2-8335-fad20f2cfef3-000000",
        "destination": [
            "bounce@simulator.amazonses.com"
        ],
        "headersTruncated": false,
        "headers": [
            {
                "name": "From",
                "value": ████████.com"
            },
            {
                "name": "To",
                "value": "bounce@simulator.amazonses.com"
            },
            {
                "name": "Subject",
                "value": "Bounced Email"
            },
            {
                "name": "MIME-Version",
                "value": "1.0"
            },
```


***Figure 3-15.** Bounced email logs from CloudWatch*

Kindly note that the log shown is a trimmed-down version of the full log. We can confirm that the test bounced mail has invoked the Lambda function.

Now, let's check how we can use the previously mentioned workflow in our emailing service.

## Workflow Visualization for Bounced Email Handling

Using the workflow mentioned in the flowchart in Figure 3-16, we can ensure that the bounced emails are handled gracefully and only valid emails are sent across.

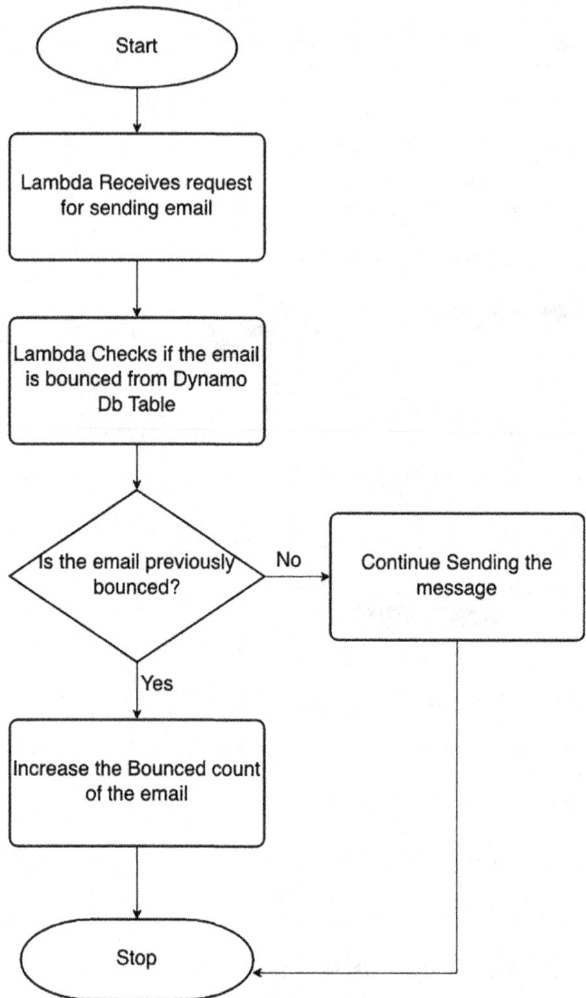


***Figure 3-16.*** *Workflow for bounced email detection*

# Event-Driven Alerting Using Serverless

Events can be used extensively to monitor systems and raise alarms accordingly. Let's consider the architecture in Figure 3-17 where we have monitoring and alerting set up for a database in RDS.

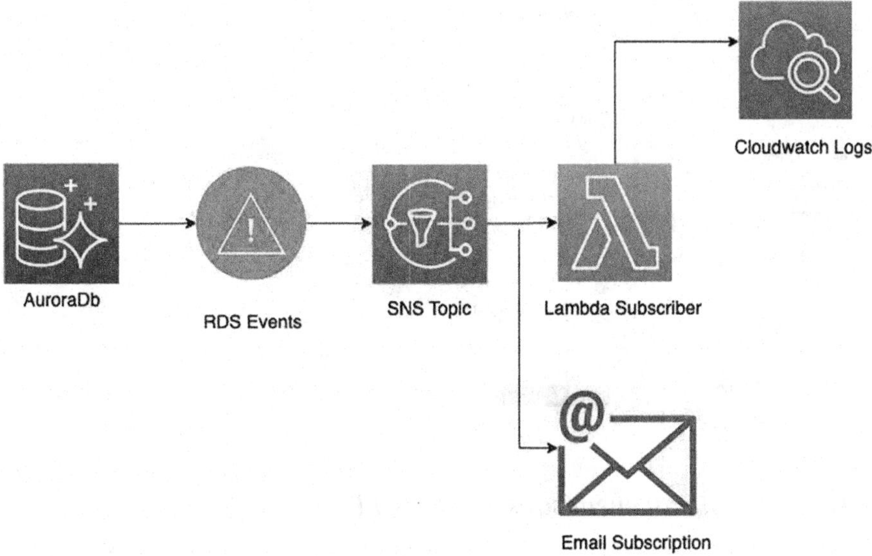


***Figure 3-17.*** *Alerting using an event-driven architecture*

We have provisioned a Aurora database. Now the use case is to get alerts whenever this database is down. We can make use of RDS event subscriptions, as shown in Figure 3-18. We can create an SNS topic and choose the RDS instance for which you need to raise notifications.

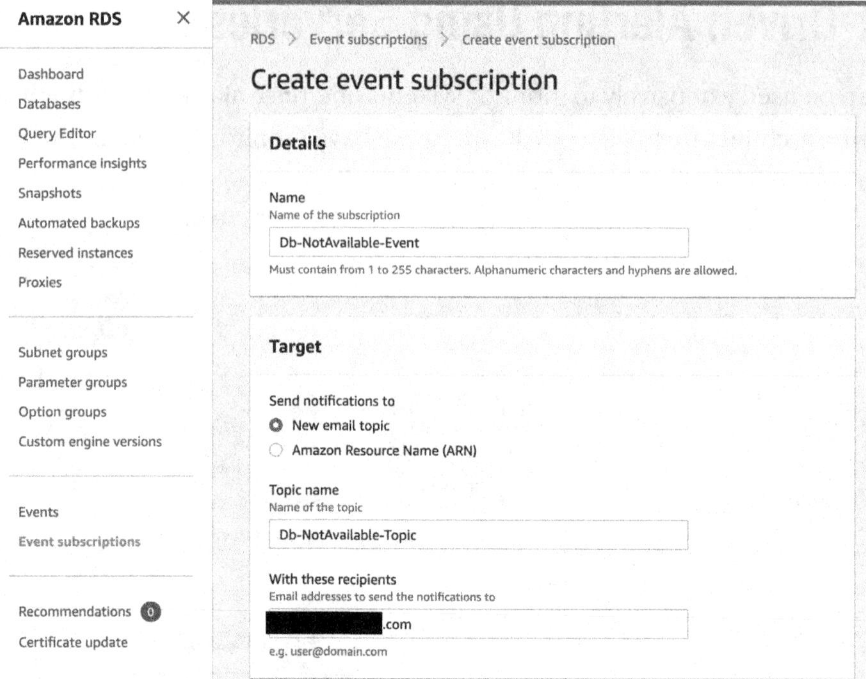


***Figure 3-18.** Creating an event subscription in RDS*

As shown in Figure 3-19, I have chosen the RDS availability/failure/maintenance events for RDS notifications.

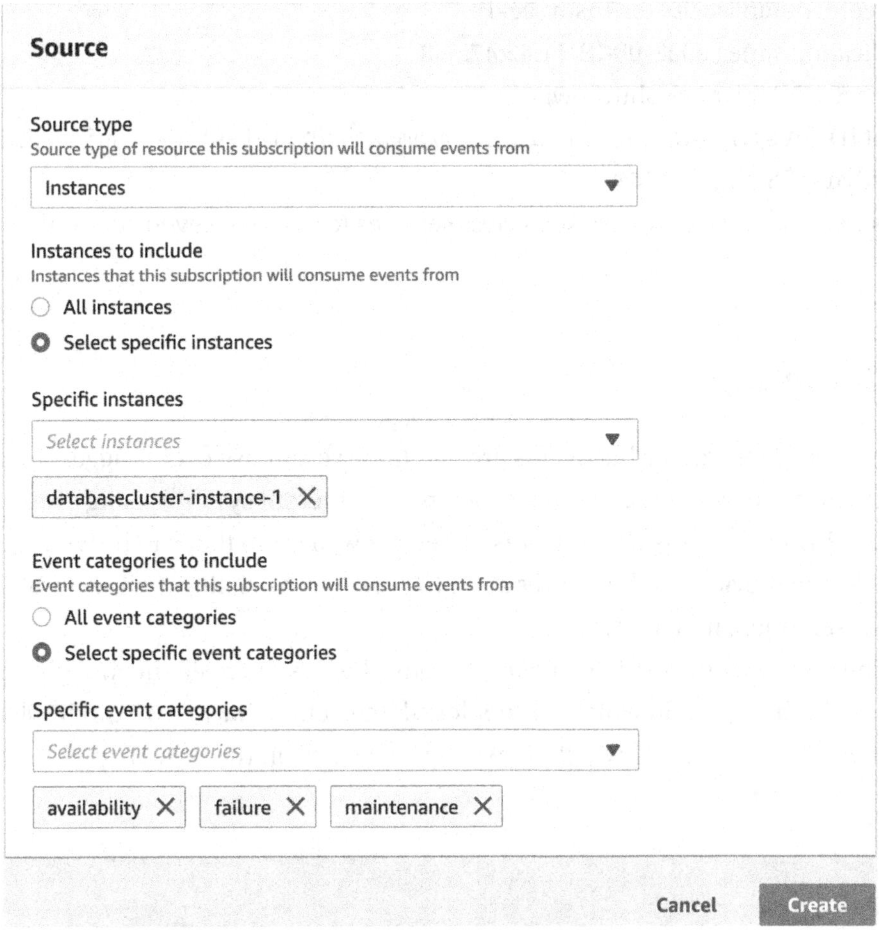

Source

Source type
Source type of resource this subscription will consume events from
Instances

Instances to include
Instances that this subscription will consume events from
All instances
Select specific instances

Specific instances
Select instances
databasecluster-instance-1

Event categories to include
Event categories that this subscription will consume events from
All event categories
Select specific event categories

Specific event categories
Select event categories
availability failure maintenance

Cancel Create

***Figure 3-19.*** *Choosing the events for notifications for the RDS instance*

After you click Create, the SNS topic, its email subscription get created. You can additionally add a Lambda subscriber and log this event to CloudWatch for auditing.

To test the aforementioned scenario, I restarted my database instance, and hence it became unavailable, and I received the following email with the event details:

From : **AWS Notifications** <no-reply@sns.amazonaws.com>

Date: Wed, Aug 31, 2022 at 5:12 PM

Subject: RDS Notification Message

To: <youremail@mailbox.com>

Event Source : db-instance

Identifier Link: `https://console.aws.amazon.com/rds/home?region=us-east-1#dbinstance:id=databasecluster-instance-1`

SourceId: databasecluster-instance-1

Notification time : 2022-08-31 11:42:47.558

Message : DB instance shutdown

Event ID : `http://docs.aws.amazon.com/AmazonRDS/latest/UserGuide/USER_Events.html#RDS-EVENT-0004`

Thus we saw how we can use serverless services to create an event-driven alerting system.

# Conclusion

In this chapter, we learned what events are and how we can use event triggers to design various event-driven systems. We can design many different systems using event-driven principles. However, in this chapter, I discussed a few of them that can be widely used. We can take the previous architectures and plug them into existing architectures as well, as they are serverless in nature.

Making a system event-driven makes it robust, but it's not resilient enough if there is an outage in the region in which it is deployed. In such scenarios, we can implement disaster recovery techniques, which we will be discussing in the next chapter.

CHAPTER 4

# Disaster Recovery Architectures

"Everything fails all the time" is a famous quote by Amazon's chief technical officer, Werner Vogels. Most AWS services have been designed for high availability, and they do rise up like a phoenix whenever a failure occurs. But what happens if an entire region or availability zone encounters an outage? In such a scenario, it would be wise to have a backup, and most distributed systems do have continuous backups. But that is just one part of making your system resilient. The bulk of the task lies in orchestrating the recovery workflow in such a way that new systems can be built immediately, with traffic being routed to the healthy systems in the event of a failure.

Over the course of this chapter, you'll learn different disaster recovery strategies, how to implement them, and how to test them.

## Introduction to Disaster Recovery Strategies

Disaster recover strategies can be classified in a number of ways. They can be based on region (multi-AZ disaster recovery), cross-region, or global disaster recovery; they can be based on RTO and RPO (active backups only, active-passive, or active-active); or they can be customized in other ways.

Let's examine a few of these a little more closely.

## Disaster Recovery Strategies Based on Region

Before we understand how to design disaster recovery plans within a region and across regions, let's understand what an availability zone is and what a region is.




J. J. Paul, *Distributed Serverless Architectures on AWS*, https://doi.org/10.1007/978-1-4842-9159-7_4

## Geographic Topology of the AWS Cloud

As you can see from Figure 4-1, the AWS cloud is divided into regions and availability zones.

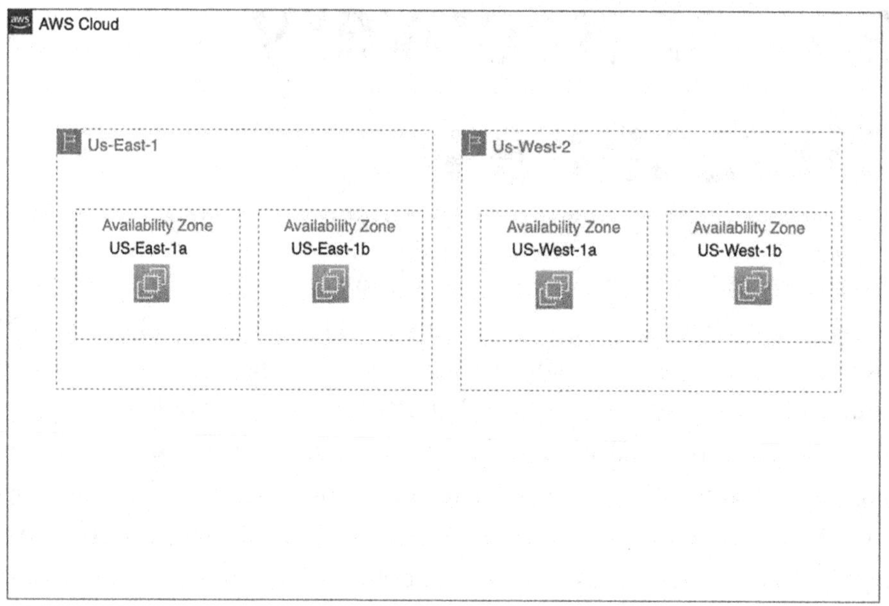


***Figure 4-1.*** *Geographic topology of the AWS cloud*

## Availability Zones

An availability zone is a set of one or more isolated data centers. These data centers have reliable networking components and constant power. In Figure 4-1, we can see two availability zones: US-East-1a and US-East-1b. In the US-East-1 zone is the North Virginia region. We can also see an EC2 instance in each availability zone. In a few AWS services such as EC2, AWS MSK brokers, AWS S3, etc., we can provision at the availability zone level. So when we provision an EC2 instance, we get the option shown in Figure 4-2 to choose the availability zone in the Networking section. Depending on our choice, the resource will get allocated in the corresponding availability zone.

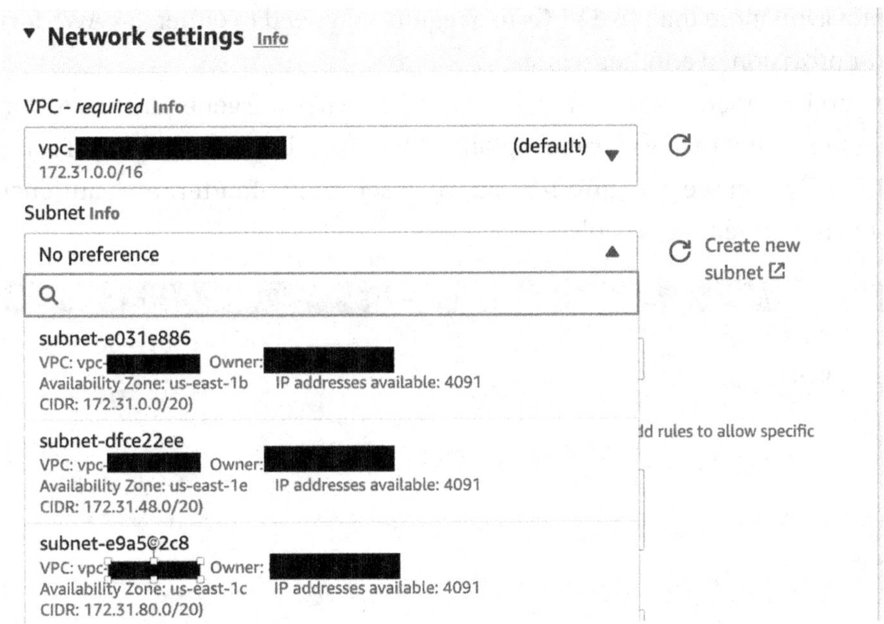

▼ Network settings Info

VPC - *required* Info

vpc- (default)
172.31.0.0/16

Subnet Info

No preference

Create new subnet

subnet-e031e886
VPC: vpc- Owner:
Availability Zone: us-east-1b IP addresses available: 4091
CIDR: 172.31.0.0/20)

subnet-dfce22ee
VPC: vpc- Owner:
Availability Zone: us-east-1e IP addresses available: 4091
CIDR: 172.31.48.0/20)

subnet-e9a5@2c8
VPC: vpc- Owner:
Availability Zone: us-east-1c IP addresses available: 4091
CIDR: 172.31.80.0/20)

***Figure 4-2.** Choosing VPC and subnet CIDR ranges in a region*

If we need to build a highly fault-tolerant application, we should distribute the application across availability zones and distribute the traffic accordingly. According to the AWS documentation, AZs are physically separated by a meaningful distance, many kilometers, from any other AZ, although all are within 100 km (60 miles) of each other. All AZs in an AWS region are interconnected with reliable and low-latency network components, and the data is encrypted as well, thus providing an additional layer of security.

## Regions

A *region* is a logical grouping of availability zones. The region is generally a physical location such as Virginia, Ohio, Frankfurt, and so on, and they are geographically separate from each other. A few services are provisioned at a regional level. For example, when we provision a secret using the Secrets Manager in the US-East-1 region, it is available across all availability zones, meaning US-East-1a, 1b, and 1c. But for other regions such as US-West-2, to access this secret, we are required to set up explicit permissions. In Figure 4-1, the separation between two regions is illustrated as well as between AZs. The service limits for most AWS services are defined at the regional level as well. For example, the default quota for the number of VPCs in a region is five. So if you want to provision more than five VPCs in a region, you need to either ask AWS for a limit increase or provision in another region.

A few services operate at the global level as well. They are generally tied to your AWS account and not to any specific region. A few examples are AWS CloudFront, IAM, Route 53, etc. We can see in Figure 4-3 that when selecting CloudFront, it automatically changes the region setting to Global.

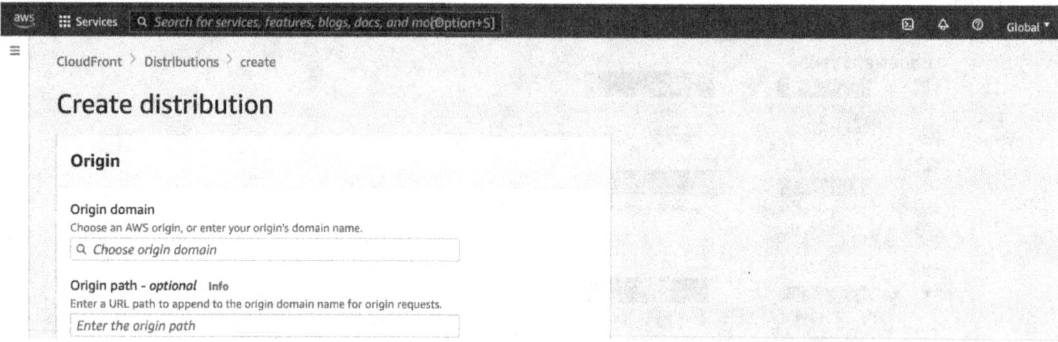


***Figure 4-3.*** *CloudFront, an example of a global service in AWS*

# Multi-AZ Disaster Recovery Strategy

The main reason for applications to be made available across AZs is to reduce the point of failure. If the same application is distributed across multiple availability zones, then even if one zone goes down, the other zones would be able to serve the content. As this book focuses on serverless architectures, let's design a multi-AZ disaster recovery for a serverless web application. Figure 4-4 shows a multi-AZ design for a serverless web application.

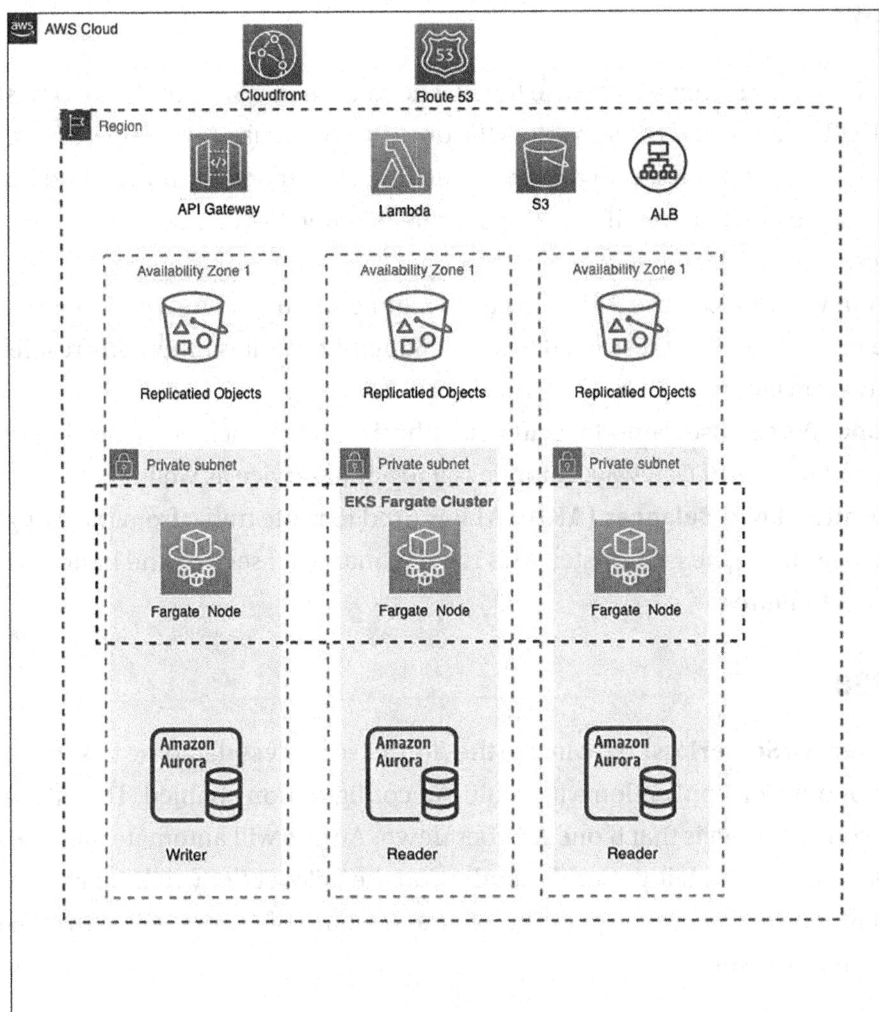


***Figure 4-4.** A serverless multi-AZ disaster recovery strategy*

## Front End

**S3 (Standard Storage Tier):** We can use the static website hosting property of S3 to host the static website content. Using the S3 standard storage tier will ensure that the objects are resilient to AZ failures as S3 replicates the objects across AZs. Hence, there is no single point of failure for your front-end application.

## Back End

**EKS with Fargate Profile:** We can use the Elastic Kubernetes Service (EKS) to host our back-end APIs, and to add the serverless flavor to it, we can use AWS Fargate instead of EC2-based worker nodes. We can spread the EKS cluster across subnets and across availability zones so that even if one AZ goes down, other AZs can cater to the back-end API requests.

**API Gateway:** We can use API Gateway to handle API traffic. As API Gateway spans the region and is not restricted to an availability zone, it is inherently resilient to availability zone failures.

**Lambda:** We can use Lambda to attach authorization to back-end APIs that are implemented using API Gateway. Lambda is a regional service as well.

**Application Load Balancer (AKB):** ALB is used to route traffic from the API gateway endpoint to nodes in the EKS cluster. ALB is a regional-level service and hence is resilient to AZ failures.

## Database

**Amazon Aurora Serverless:** We can use the Aurora serverless database to serve as the database for our web application with multi-AZ configuration enabled. The advantage of multi-AZ configuration is that if one AZ goes down, Aurora will automate failover to the replica in another availability zone depending on the failover tier you have chosen.

Let's emulate a disaster scenario and see the scenario of Aurora failing over to the replica cluster in action.

**Step 1:**

Create an Aurora multi-AZ configuration by choosing the multi-AZ option, as demonstrated in Figure 4-5.

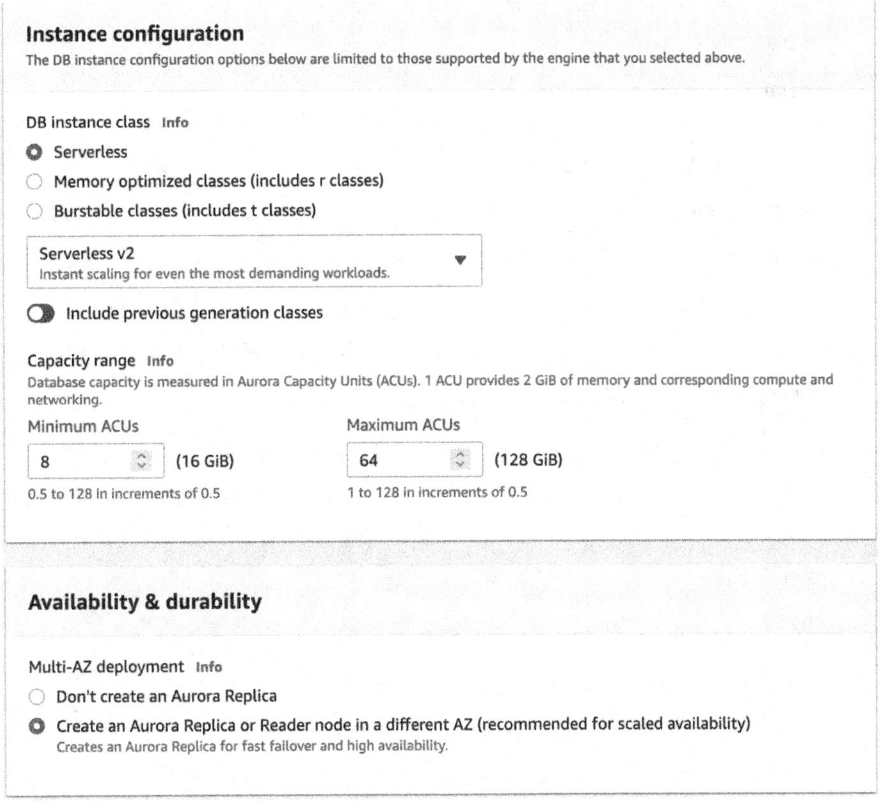

***Figure 4-5.*** *Aurora multi-AZ configuration*

**Step 2:**

If you want more resilience and performance, you can add replicas and choose the appropriate tier for failover, as shown in Figure 4-6.

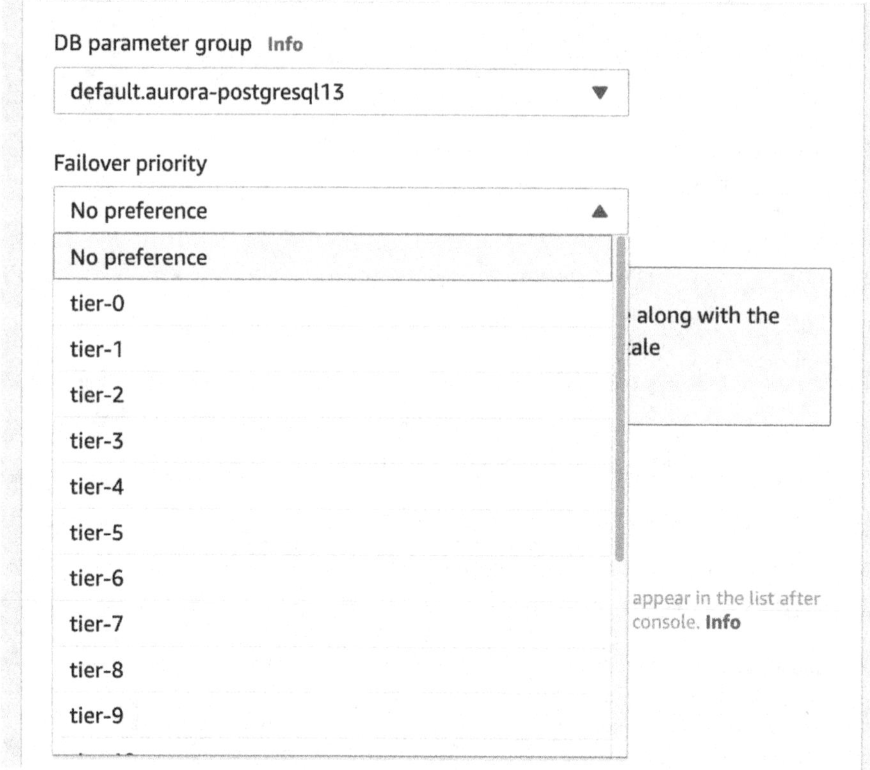

***Figure 4-6.** Adding resiliency to an Aurora cluster by assigning tiers*

In the event of a failover, the read replica with the highest priority, i.e., the lowest tier, is promoted first.

**Step 3:**

Ensure that both instances are active, as shown in Figure 4-7.

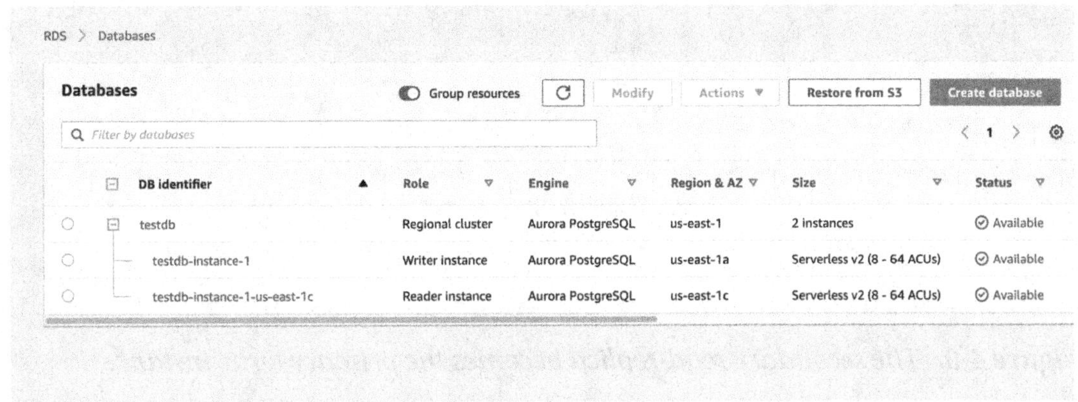


***Figure 4-7.*** *Aurora database cluster view*

**Step 4:**

Delete the primary instance to create a failover event, as shown in Figure 4-8.

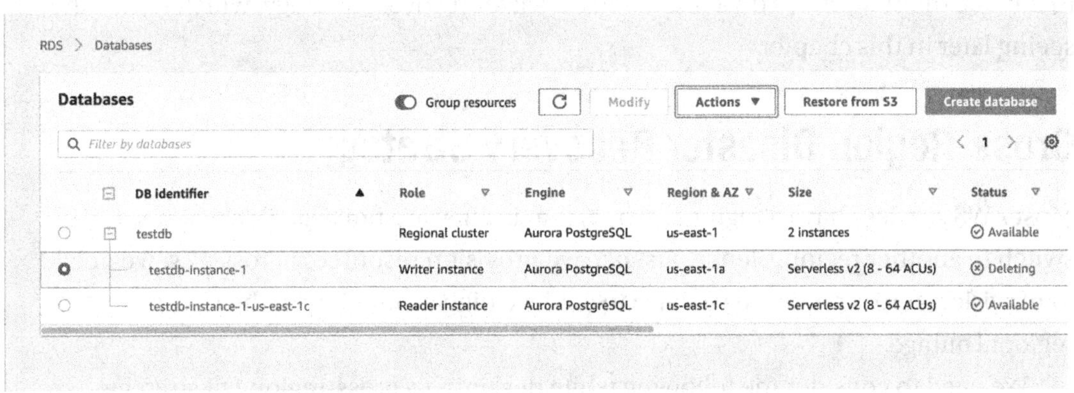


***Figure 4-8.*** *Triggering failover*

**Step 5:**

Notice that the Aurora read replica in US-East-1c is now the primary instance and the failover is successful to the replica, as shown in Figure 4-9.

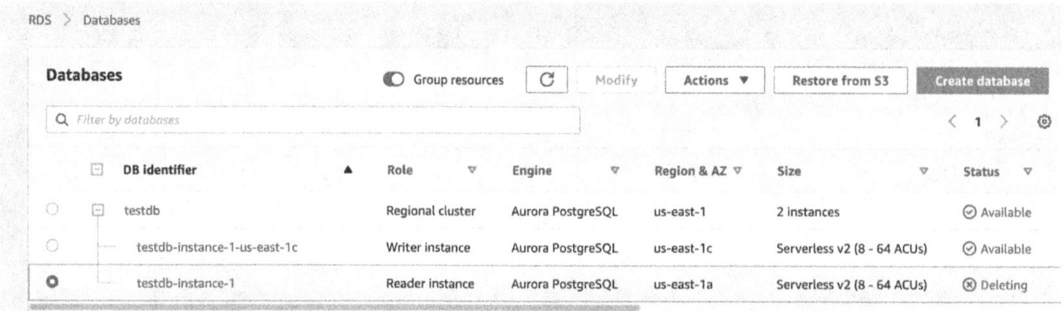


***Figure 4-9.** The secondary read-replica becomes the primary write instance*

Hence, we can see from the previous example that Aurora is highly resilient to failures and is a good candidate for a disaster recovery strategy.

The content delivery service AWS CloudFront and the AWS DNS service Route 53 are global services, and we need to include them in our DR strategy. However, we will have to include them when we do a multicloud disaster recovery strategy, which we will be seeing later in this chapter.

# Cross-Region Disaster Recovery Strategy

Most AWS services have a regional scope; that is, they are not available when we switch to another region. Hence, just like we provision resources across AZs, we need to provision across regions if we have to achieve high availability in the case of a regional outage.

We need to consider the following while designing a cross-region DR strategy:

- *Configuration*: If you require your resources in both regions to always be available, you can use an active-active configuration, where data is constantly in sync with both regions. Otherwise, you can use an active-passive configuration where there would be some downtime before the failover region starts serving traffic. With active-active, the cost would be higher as data transfer rates and keeping services in an active state would incur costs.

- *Failover policies*: We need to decide upon the scenarios in which a failover should be triggered. Either we can keep this via CloudWatch alarms and link the state of the alarms to Health Checks or we can configure Health Checks to check endpoints.

Let's consider an active-active configuration serverless architecture for a cross-region replica, as shown in Figure 4-10.

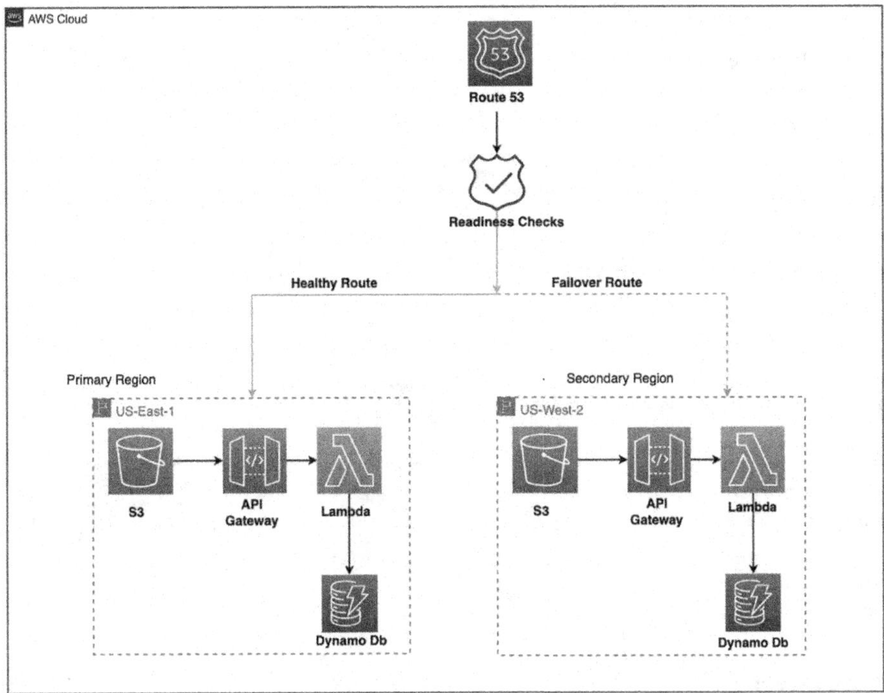


***Figure 4-10.*** *Cross-region DR strategy using serverless*

Let's implement the DR strategy for the following areas.

## Front-End DR Implementation

We are hosting the front-end code using the S3 bucket's static website hosting feature. Although S3 has an availability and durability of more than 99 percent, in the case of regional outages, S3 can be unavailable as well. We can build resiliency into S3 across regions by implementing the following steps:

**Step1: Enable Cross-Region Replication for the S3 Bucket**

Cross-region replication enables the bucket contents to be replicated across regions and across accounts. We need to set up replication rules on the bucket, and it will start replicating asynchronously. See Figure 4-11.

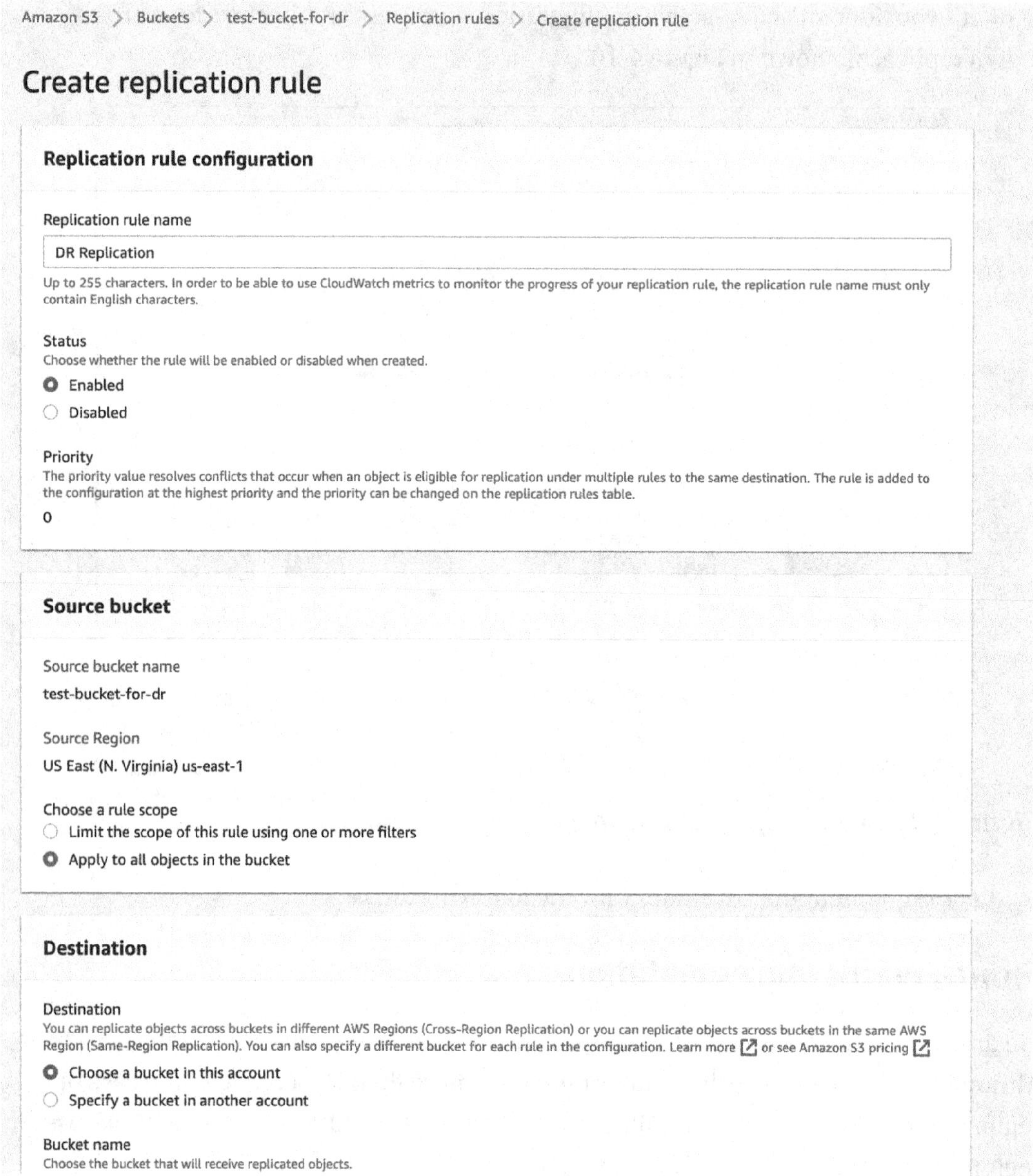

Amazon S3 > Buckets > test-bucket-for-dr > Replication rules > Create replication rule

Create replication rule

Replication rule configuration

Replication rule name

DR Replication

Up to 255 characters. In order to be able to use CloudWatch metrics to monitor the progress of your replication rule, the replication rule name must only contain English characters.

Status

Choose whether the rule will be enabled or disabled when created.

Enabled

Disabled

Priority

The priority value resolves conflicts that occur when an object is eligible for replication under multiple rules to the same destination. The rule is added to the configuration at the highest priority and the priority can be changed on the replication rules table.

0

Source bucket

Source bucket name

test-bucket-for-dr

Source Region

US East (N. Virginia) us-east-1

Choose a rule scope

Limit the scope of this rule using one or more filters

Apply to all objects in the bucket

Destination

Destination

You can replicate objects across buckets in different AWS Regions (Cross-Region Replication) or you can replicate objects across buckets in the same AWS Region (Same-Region Replication). You can also specify a different bucket for each rule in the configuration. Learn more or see Amazon S3 pricing

Choose a bucket in this account

Specify a bucket in another account

Bucket name

Choose the bucket that will receive replicated objects.

***Figure 4-11.** Replication rule configuration for S3*

You need to add an IAM role as well to enable cross-region replication. Add the following trust policy to the IAM role you are creating:

```
{
    "Version": "2012-10-17",
```

```
    "Statement": [
    {
        "Effect": "Allow",
        "Principal": {
        "Service": "s3.amazonaws.com"
        },
        "Action": "sts:AssumeRole"
    }
    ]
}
```

Create a new policy to allow replication and add the following lines to the policy. In addition, replace the source and destination bucket's arn value with the respective bucket ARNs:

```
{
    "Version": "2012-10-17",
    "Statement": [
    {
        "Effect": "Allow",
        "Action": [
        "s3:GetReplicationConfiguration",
        "s3:ListBucket"
        ],
        "Resource": [
        "arn:aws:s3:::sourcebucket/*"
        ]
    },
    {
        "Effect": "Allow",
        "Action": [
        "s3:GetObjectVersionForReplication",
        "s3:GetObjectVersionAcl",
        "s3:GetObjectVersionTagging"
        ],
        "Resource": [
        "arn:aws:s3:::sourcebucket/*"
```

```
            ]
        },
        {
            "Effect": "Allow",
            "Action": [
            "s3:ReplicateObject",
            "s3:ReplicateDelete",
            "s3:ReplicateTags"
            ],
            "Resource": "arn:aws:s3:::destinationbucket/*"
        }
        ]
}
```

Once the role is selected and the replication rule is active, we can see that the new objects will be automatically replicated, as shown in Figure 4-12.

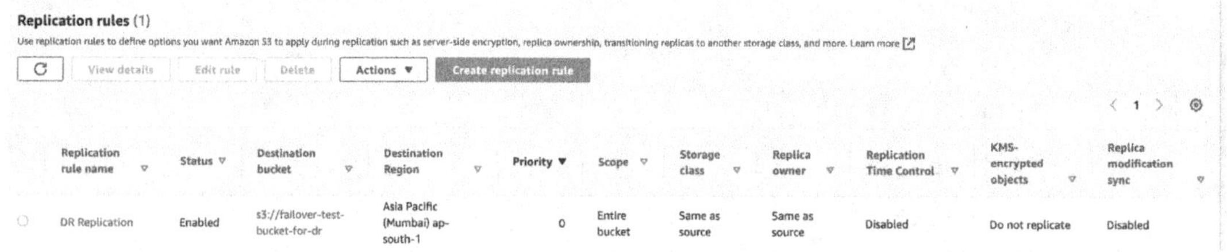


***Figure 4-12.** Replication rule configuration for the S3 bucket*

---

**Note** It is ideal to create the replication rules before any objects are uploaded. However, we can run a batch job as well to replicate existing objects. For ease of implementation, I have made the S3 bucket publicly accessible.

---

To test this, I uploaded a file called `index2.html` to my source bucket in US-East-1 at 17:59, as you can see in Figure 4-13.

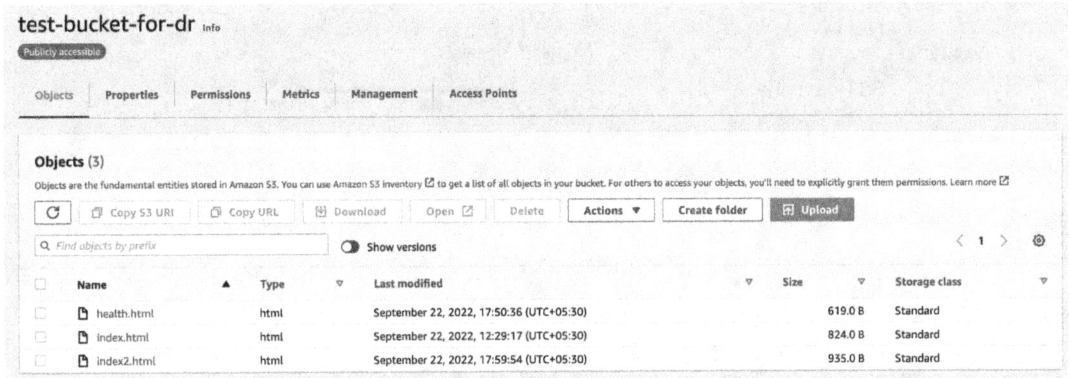


***Figure 4-13.*** *Testing data replication from the primary bucket in US-East-1*

It was replicated to the destination bucket in AP-South-1 at 17:59 itself, as in Figure 4-14.

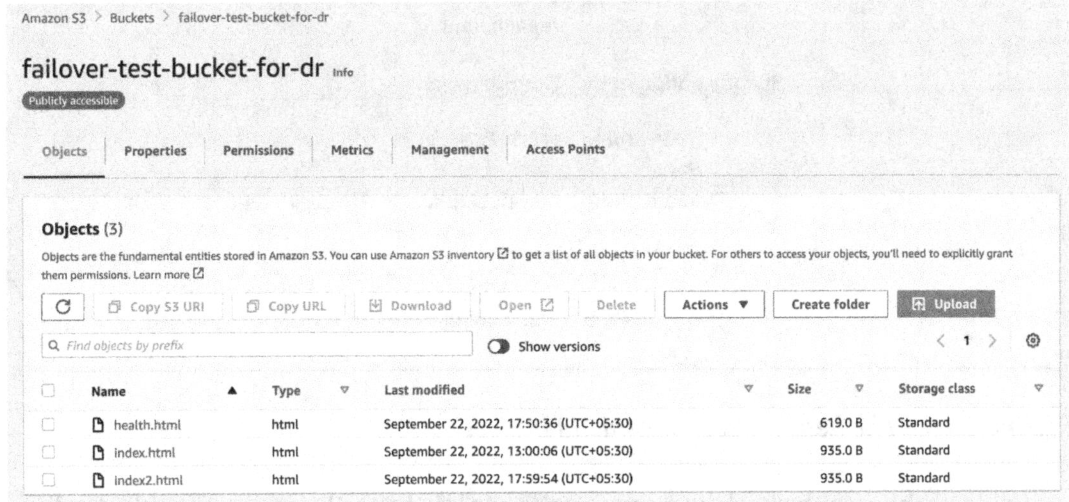


***Figure 4-14.*** *Data succesfully replicated in the secondary bucket in AP-South-1*

#### Step 2: Create an S3 Health Check for the Primary Region

Now that we have enabled cross-region replication, we need to check for the availability of the S3 bucket in the primary region. So, let's create a health check and keep the `health.html` file in our S3 website as the health check endpoint, as shown in Figure 4-15.

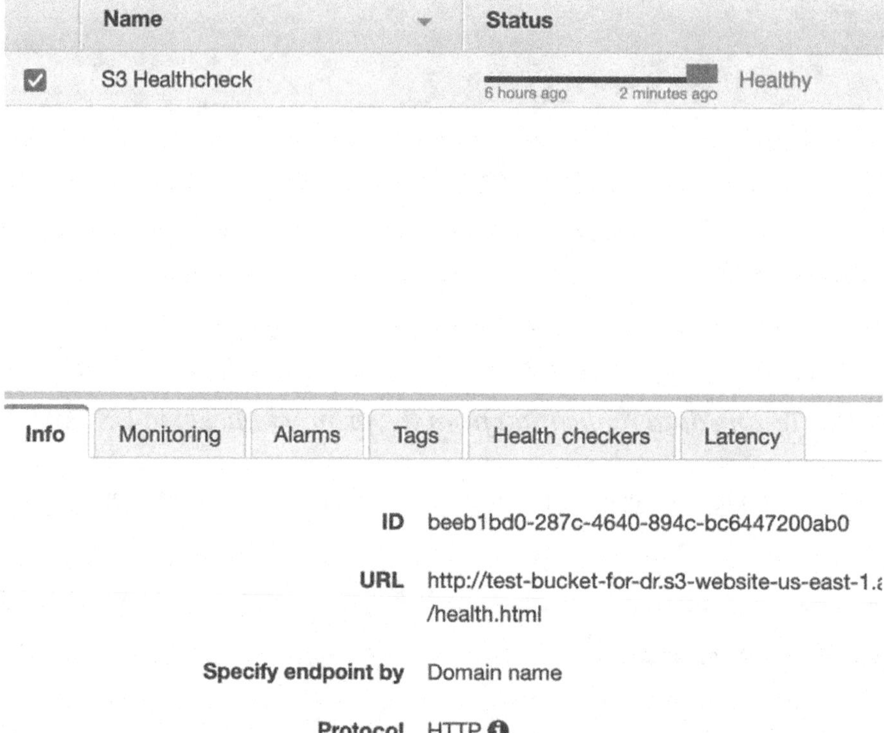


***Figure 4-15.*** *The health check for the S3 bucket*

I did test this health check by removing the `health.html` file, and the health check failed. Once I uploaded the object again, it became successful. So, we are good with the health check now.

**Step 3: Create a Route 53 CNAME Record with a Failover Routing Policy**

Now that we have the health checks in place, we need to create two CNAME records with the front-end domain name and point them to the respective S3 buckets in US-East-1 and AP-South-1, as shown in Figure 4-16.

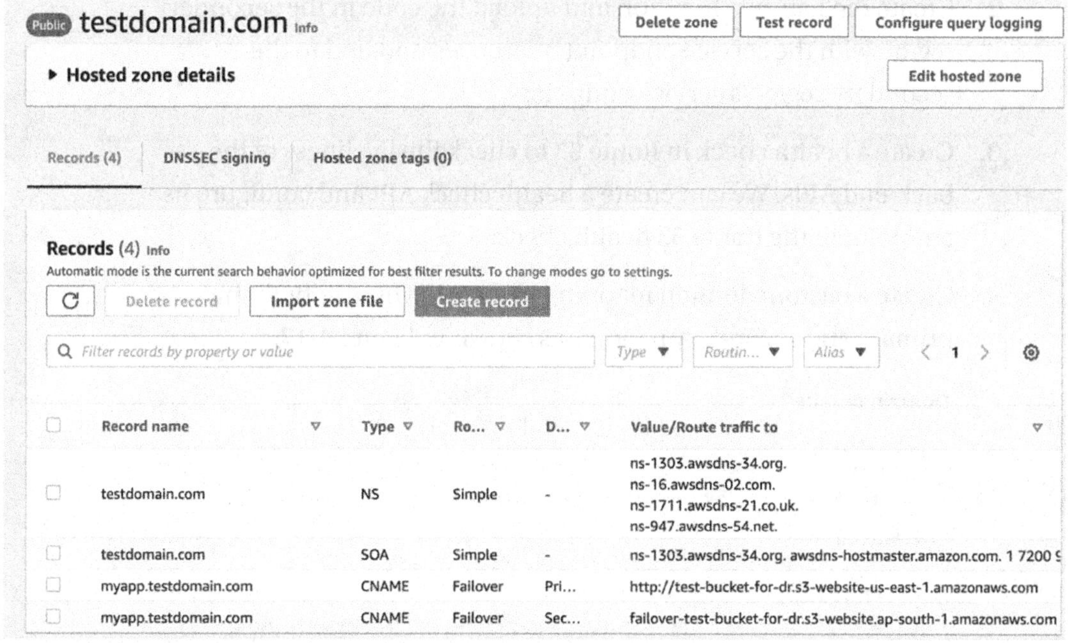


***Figure 4-16.*** *Route 53 domains for S3 bucket*

Now whenever we hit the domain `myapp.testdomain.com`, Route 53 will check the failover routing policy and route the traffic accordingly. If the US-East-1 Bucket is not available, the traffic will be served from AP-South-1.

---

**Note** In production, it is better to choose your DR regions in close proximity to the primary region to minimize latency.

---

## Back-End DR Implementation

The back end of the architecture in Figure 4-10 consists of an API gateway integrated with the Lambda function. If we need these services to be available in an active-active configuration, we need to perform the following steps:

1. Create the API gateway in the secondary region, which is AP-South-1 here.

2. Create the Lambda function and upload the code in the secondary region with the service endpoint references updated to the secondary region's service endpoints.

3. Create a health check in Route 53 to check the liveliness of the back-end APIs. We can create a health check API and configure its endpoint in the Route 53 health check.

4. Create a custom domain mapping to the API URLs in both the primary and secondary regions, as shown in Figure 4-17.

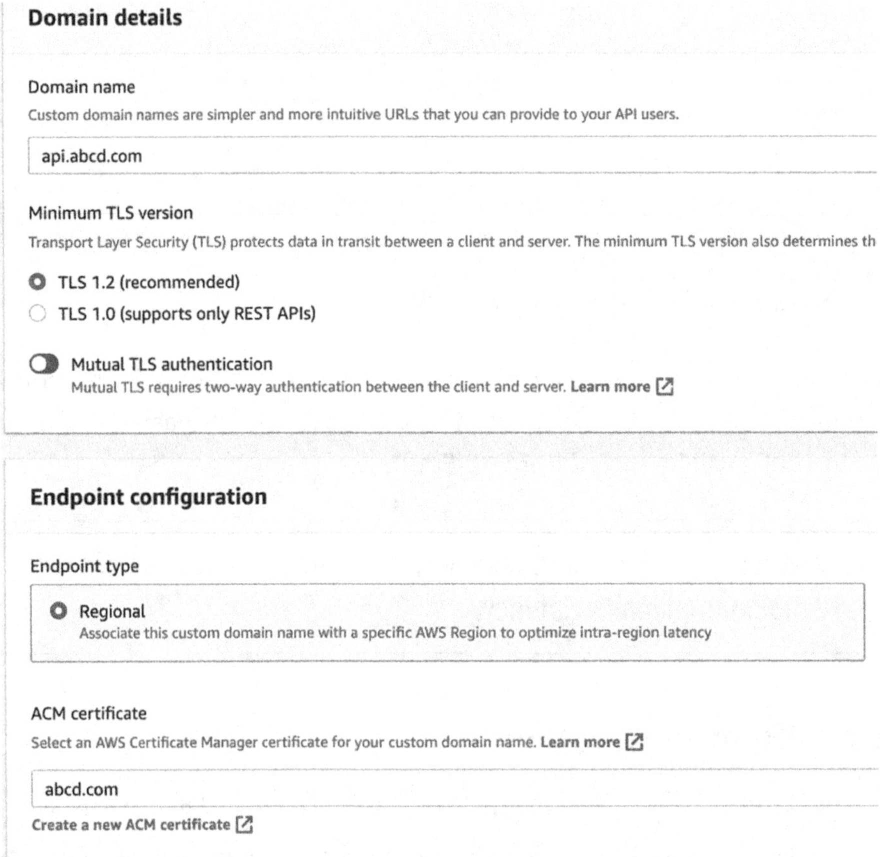

Domain details

Domain name

Custom domain names are simpler and more intuitive URLs that you can provide to your API users.

api.abcd.com

Minimum TLS version

Transport Layer Security (TLS) protects data in transit between a client and server. The minimum TLS version also determines th

TLS 1.2 (recommended)

TLS 1.0 (supports only REST APIs)

Mutual TLS authentication

Mutual TLS requires two-way authentication between the client and server. Learn more

Endpoint configuration

Endpoint type

Regional

Associate this custom domain name with a specific AWS Region to optimize intra-region latency

ACM certificate

Select an AWS Certificate Manager certificate for your custom domain name. Learn more

abcd.com

Create a new ACM certificate

***Figure 4-17.*** *Custom domain mapping for API URLs*

5. Create CNAME records for the URLs using a failover routing policy, as we did for S3; this is shown in Figure 4-18.

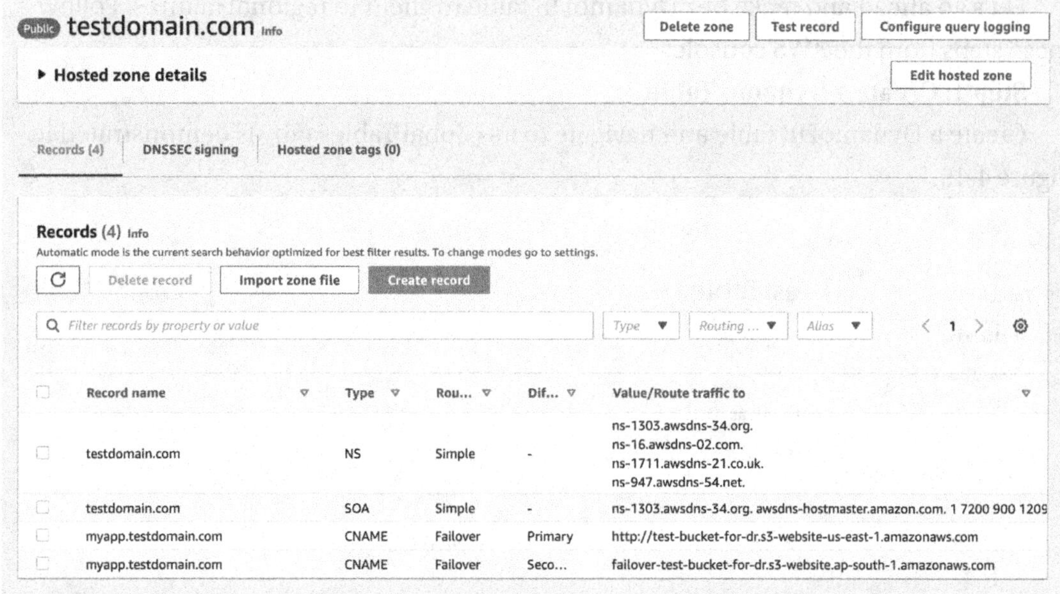


***Figure 4-18.*** *Route 53 domain mapping*

Once the previous steps are completed, our back-end services are resilient to disaster, and they can actively serve traffic from the AP-South-1 region if the API Gateway service is unavailable in the primary region, i.e., US-East-1.

## Serverless Database Disaster Recovery Implementation

In our architecture, we are using DynamoDB as the database. To make it resilient for regional failures, we can use the global tables feature.

Global tables provide us with a fully managed, multiregion, and multi-active database. We can replicate the DynamoDB global tables across multiple AWS regions.

In the event of a regional outage, the reads and writes to the table can be done from a different region to the read replica. Your application can redirect to a different region and perform reads and writes against a different replica table. As per the AWS documentation, DynamoDB keeps track of any writes that have been performed but have not yet been propagated to all of the replica tables. When the region comes back online, DynamoDB resumes propagating any pending writes from that region to the replica tables in other regions and vice versa. Also, to enable cross-region replication, AWS enables DynamoDB streams, which capture item-level modifications in Dynamo DB tables, when we add a cross-region replica for the table.

Let's go ahead and make our DynamoDB table resilient to regional failures. Follow these steps from the AWS console:

**Step 1: Create a Dynamo Table**

Create a DynamoDB table and navigate to its Global Tables tab, as demonstrated in Figure 4-19.

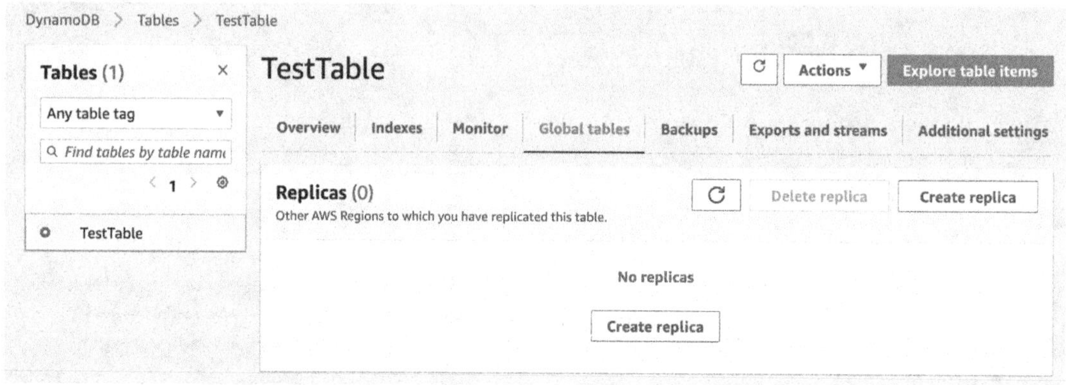


***Figure 4-19.** DynamoDB table creation*

**Step 2: Create a Replica**

Click Create Replica and choose your region. I have chosen the US-East-1 region. The replica table gets created, as shown in Figure 4-20.

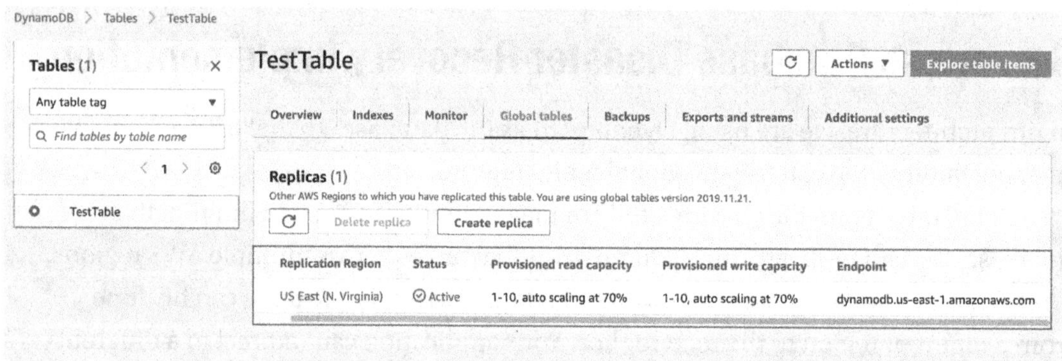


***Figure 4-20.** Creation of replica table*

**Step 3: Verify the Replication**

Verify the items in the primary table and the replica and ensure that all items are replicated. Figure 4-21 shows the list of items in the primary table in the Mumbai region.

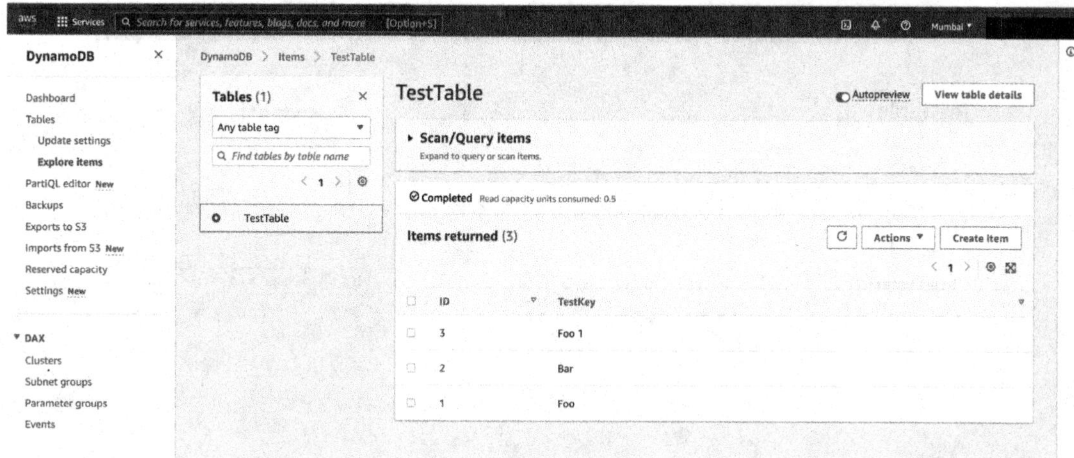


*Figure 4-21. Verifying the existing data replication*

**Step 4: Verify the New Data Replication**

Add a new item to the primary and ensure that it is replicated.

To verify this step, I am adding an item with an ID of 4, as shown in Figure 4-22.

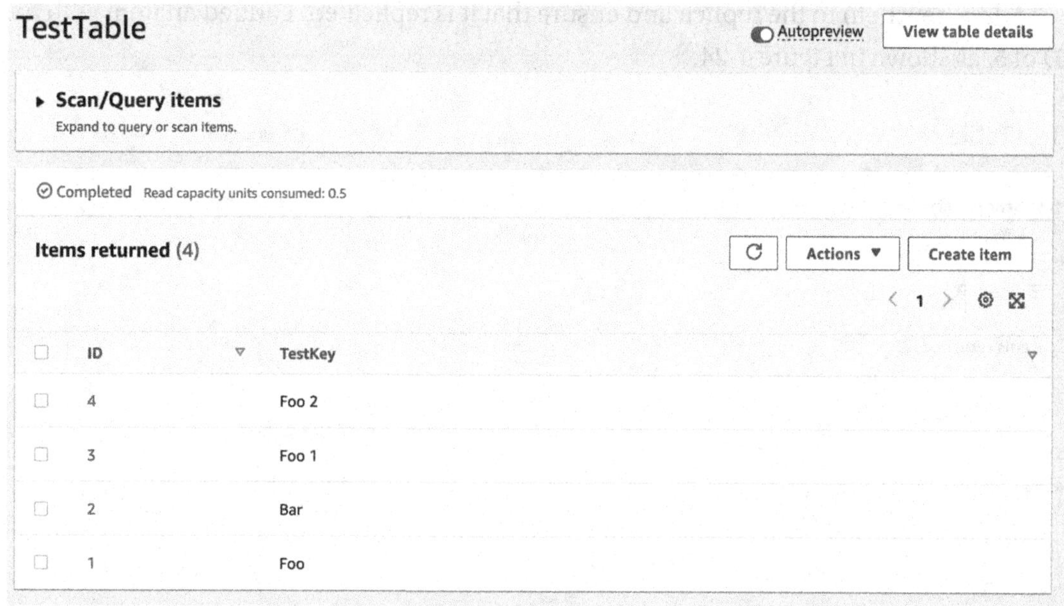


*Figure 4-22. Adding an item with an ID of 4*

Notice that all items in the test table in the Mumbai region have been replicated to the replica table in US-East-1, as shown in Figure 4-23.

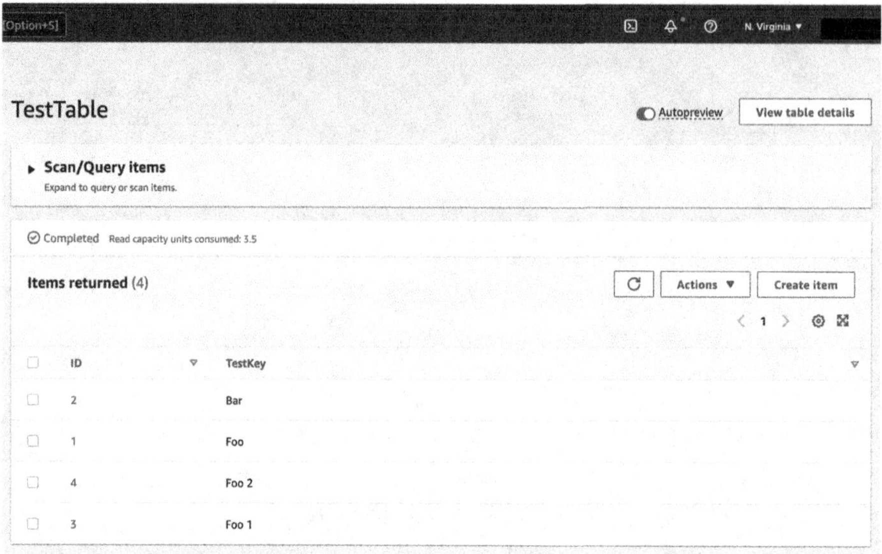


***Figure 4-23.** Data replicated to the replica table*

### Step 5: Verify Again with More Data

Add a new item to the replica and ensure that it is replicated. I added an item with an ID of 5, as shown in Figure 4-24.

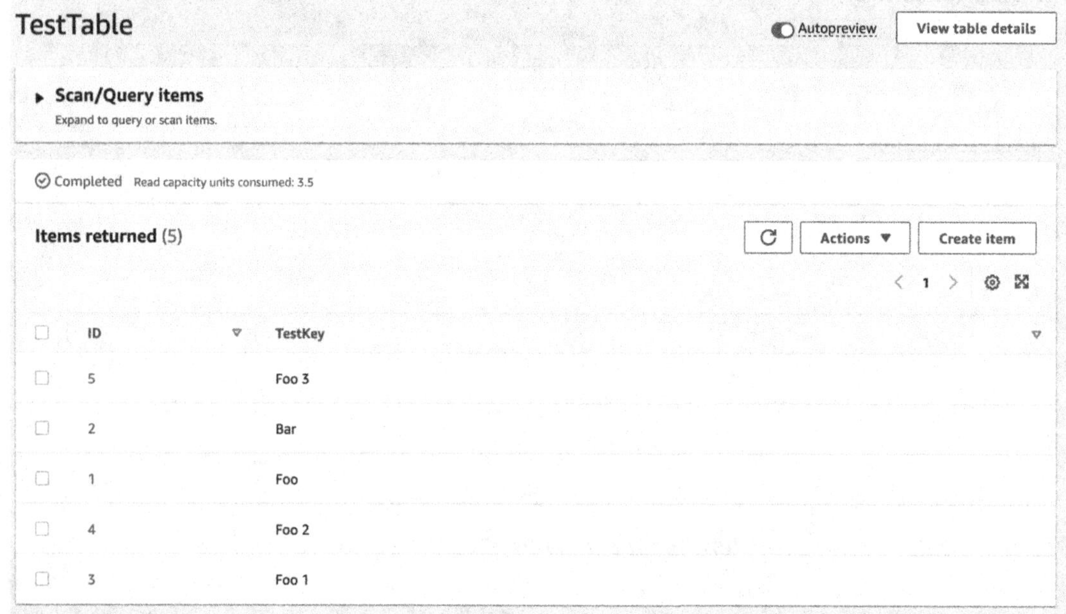


***Figure 4-24.** Reverifying data replication by inserting more items*

Notice that the new item has been replicated into the primary table in the AP-South-1 region as well, as shown in Figure 4-25.

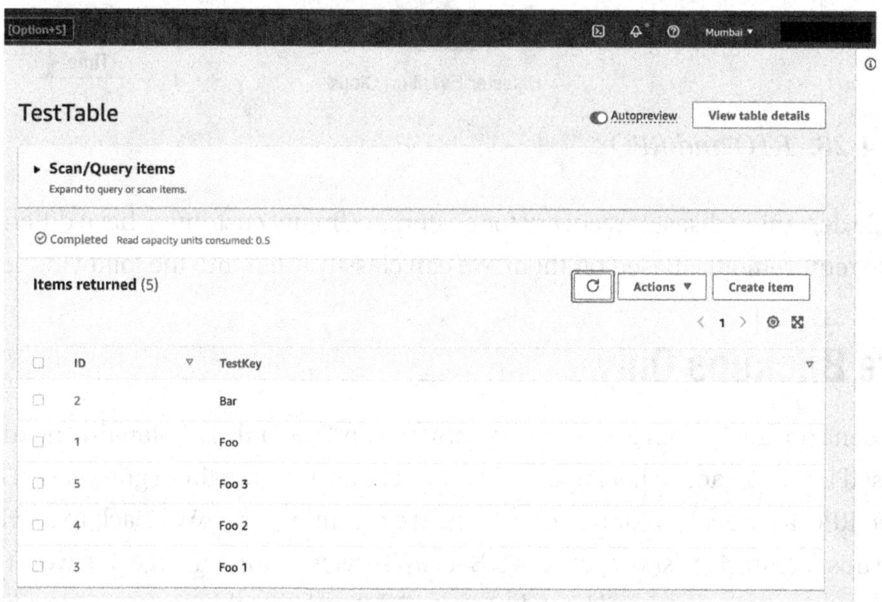


***Figure 4-25.*** *Data successfully replicated to the table in AP-South-1*

Thus, we can see that the DynamoDB global tables feature helps us to achieve resiliency at the cross-region level from the database tier. We can use Aurora global tables as well for database layer replication, but since we are dealing with serverless architectures in this book, we have used DynamoDB.

# Disaster Recovery Strategy Based on RTO and RPO

Let's understand what RTO and RPO are.

- The *recovery time objective* (RTO) indicates the downtime that the system requires to return to its normal state in the case of an outage.
- The *recovery point objective* (RPO) indicates the amount of data loss the system can accommodate in the event of a disaster. Figure 4-26 illustrates this.

***Figure 4-26.*** *RTO and RPO*

While designing disaster recovery for customers, many customers have different RTO and RPO requirements. Based on them, we can classify them into the following sections.

## Active Backups Only

In this scenario, the system is not mission critical, and the only DR plan that needs to be devised is to take active backups of all resources and restore them gradually. The RTO and RPO are very low for these systems. We can utilize the AWS Backup service to achieve this. Figure 4-27 shows the AWS Backup service's landing page. We won't be explaining this service in detail here, but on a high level it enables us to create a backup of AWS resources within a region, and we can store the backup in a backup vault. Also, we can customize the backups, define daily retention periods, and so on.

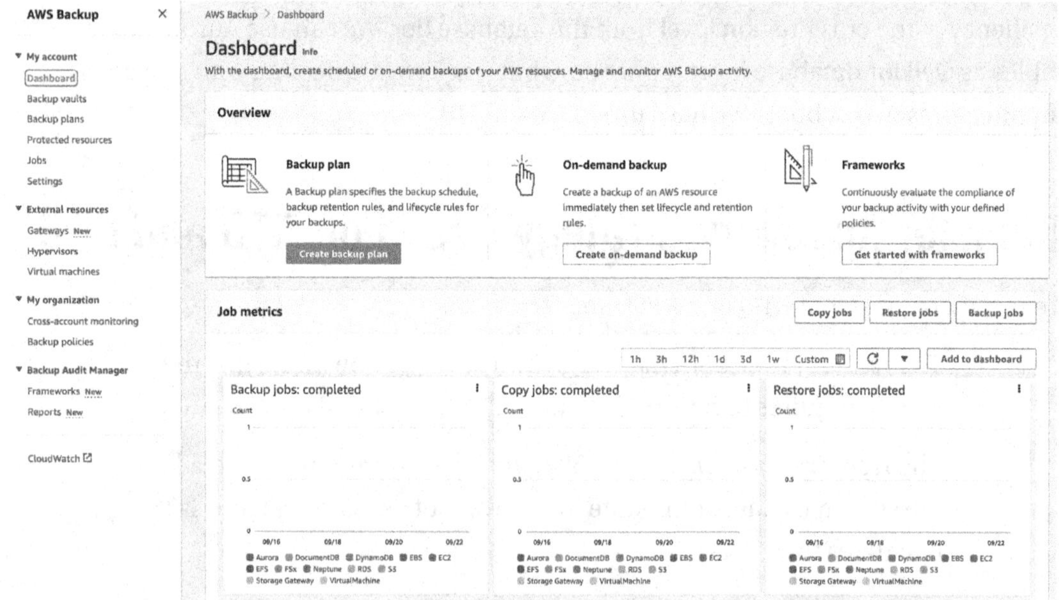


***Figure 4-27.*** *The dashboard of the AWS Backup service*

## Active-Active Configuration

This configuration has the highest RTO and RPO and the highest cost for running the disaster recovery environment. Systems in these configurations can hardly be down, so all the components across regions must be in their active state, and data and objects must be replicated always. In the case of disaster, the secondary system must be able to serve traffic within two to three minutes. We already saw an example of this architecture in Figure 4-10, in the "Cross-Region Disaster Recovery Strategy" section. The same configuration can be placed within a region as well.

## Active-Passive Configuration

This configuration is similar to the active-active configuration but has a slightly lower RTO and RPO. In the case of a disaster, it has a few minutes of downtime before it starts serving live traffic. In this strategy, services like EC2, RDS, and others will be provisioned, but they won't be ready to serve traffic. If a disaster occurs, then we could manually make these services active. Hence, the cost of running this architecture is lower than an active-active configuration.

# Conclusion

In this chapter, you learned how to design serverless systems in the event of a disaster, including strategies on the AZ level and the cross-region level. Additionally, you learned how to design disaster recovery strategies for the front end, back end, and databases in serverless architectures. Lastly, we covered disaster recovery scenarios based on RTO and RPO requirements.

In the next chapter, you will learn about data-platform-based architectures and how to build them using serverless components.

# CHAPTER 5

# Serverless Data Platforms

Over the past several years, the amount of data generated by systems around the world has increased, and continues to increase at an exponential rate. Collecting, processing, and analyzing this data at scale has become an absolute necessity for organizations around the world.

In this chapter, we'll cover the following topics:

- What a data platform is
- Advantages of running a data platform on the cloud
- Understanding the serverless data platform on AWS
- Building a serverless data analytics application
- Leveraging AWS Data Pipeline to build a data pipeline

## Overview of Data Platforms

A *data platform* is an end-to-end solution for ingesting, storing, processing, and visualizing data at scale. It is a place where data can be modeled to suit various business requirements such as making insights, defining data access patterns, etc. In essence, it consists of steps starting at the stage when data is collected and ingested to the stage where we can view this data in a structured and insightful manner.

Figure 5-1 shows what a data platform looks like at a high level.

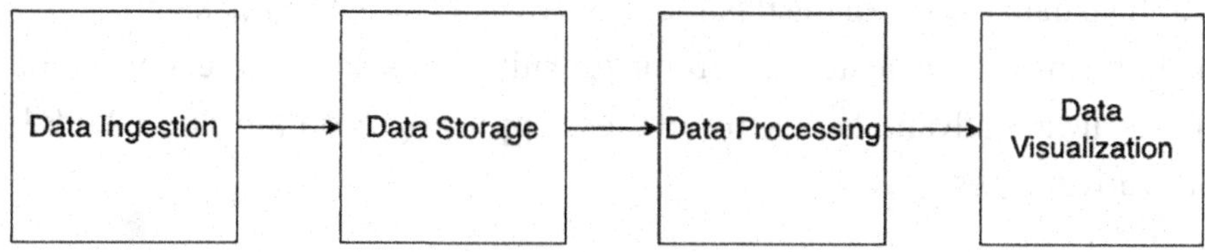


***Figure 5-1.*** *Data platform at a high level*




J. J. Paul, *Distributed Serverless Architectures on AWS*, https://doi.org/10.1007/978-1-4842-9159-7_5

Let's take a look at each of these elements and examine them in depth.

## Data Ingestion

Data ingestion involves ingesting data collected from various sources such as IoT devices, mobile devices, logs, etc., in real time or near real time. This is the first step of data processing, and we should ensure the services we are using for ingestion must be able to handle data ingestion at scale; otherwise, we end up losing data in the process. A few examples of data ingestion services in AWS are Kinesis, AWS Glue, AWS MSK, AWS DMS, etc. The responsibility of the ingestion layer is to collect data and ingest it into the AWS ecosystem so that a wide variety of AWS services can consume it.

## Data Storage

We need a persistent storage service for the data before processing (data lakes) and after processing (data warehousing). We use services such as AWS S3, AWS Lake Formation, Amazon Redshift, and DynamoDB for data storage in AWS.

## Data Processing

In this stage, the data is processed and made ready for consumption and visualization. This involves cleaning, sorting, normalizing, and transforming data as per the requirements. We can use multiple AWS services such as AWS Glue, AWS EMR, AWS Data Pipeline, etc., for processing.

## Data Visualization

The processed data needs to be consumed and stored in a data warehouse where it can be readily visualized. We can use AWS Redshift for this purpose. To derive insights from this data and visualize them using dashboards, we can use AWS QuickSight.

Data platforms can be hosted on-premises with stand-alone servers or on the cloud. However, it is always advantageous to run these applications on the cloud. Let's look at a few of these advantages.

## Advantages of Running Data Platforms on the Cloud

We will be discussing the advantages of running data platforms on the cloud in terms of cost, scalability, and availability when compared with on-premise data platforms.

- *Cost*: As most services are available in a pay-per-use cost model, running a data platform on the cloud is way cheaper as we don't have to pay for running the services 24/7, monitoring, and maintenance.
- *Scalability*: Services such as AWS Glue, Redshift, etc., can be scaled dynamically to large values, and they can be scaled down easily as well. This is in stark contrast to scaling resources on-premises, as it takes at times days to scale up the infrastructure.
- *Availability*: Running your data platforms on the cloud ensures that your data is readily available for consumption even in the case of a disaster or outage as the data can be replicated into other regions easily in a distributed manner. This level of availability architecture is quite difficult to implement in data platforms hosted on-premises.

Now that we have familiarized ourselves with what a data platform looks like, let's explore how can set up a serverless data platform on AWS.

## Serverless Data Platform on AWS

The serverless data platform on AWS is quite large, and it has serverless services for each layer of the data platform. Figure 5-2 shows the serverless services we can use for each layer.

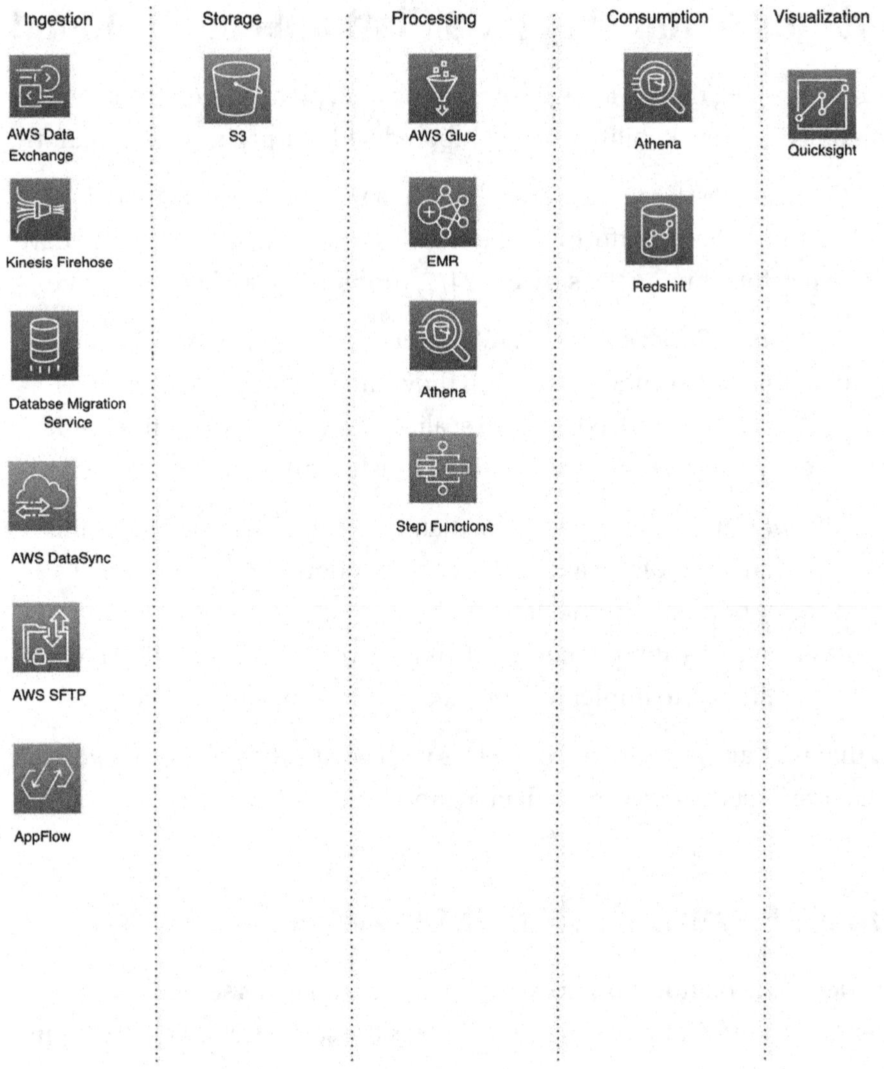


***Figure 5-2.*** *Serverless data platform on AWS*

# Data Ingestion Services

We already discussed data ingestion while giving an overview of data platforms at the beginning of the chapter. Now let's look at the serverless services that will enable us to carry out data ingestion.

## AWS Data Exchange

AWS Data Exchange enables you to ingest data from third-party applications directly into the data lake landing zone in Amazon S3.

## Kinesis Data Firehose

Kinesis Data Firehose can be used to collect streaming data from internal and external sources. Kinesis Firehose can batch the streams, process them, compress them, and encrypt them, and it can store them as S3 objects in the landing zone of an S3 data lake.

Kinesis Data Firehose can also deliver streaming data to Amazon Redshift, Amazon OpenSearch Service, Splunk, and any custom HTTP endpoint or HTTP endpoints owned by supported third-party service providers, such as Datadog, MongoDB, etc.

Figure 5-3 shows a simple implementation of Kinesis Data Firehose, where data that is streamed from multiple sources gets transformed through Kinesis Data Firehose and is persisted in an S3 bucket.

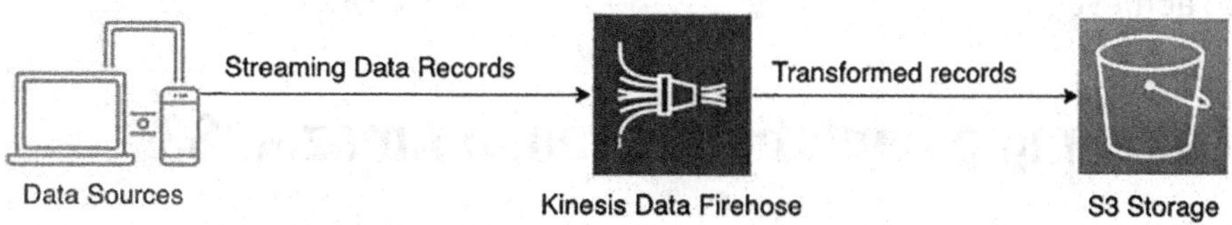


***Figure 5-3.*** *A Kinesis Data Firehose implementation*

## Database Migration Service

The Database Migration Service is used to migrate data across databases. But the same service can be used to ingest data into an S3 data lake as well by keeping the destination as the S3 lake, importing data, and replicating ongoing changes.

## AWS DataSync

We can use AWS DataSync to ingest millions of files from the Network File System (NFS) and Server Message Block (SMB)-enabled NAS devices into the data lake landing zone in S3. DataSync can perform file transfers and can synchronize changed files into the data lake.

## AWS SFTP

The AWS Transfer Family is a serverless, highly available, and scalable service that supports secure FTP endpoints and natively integrates with Amazon S3. We can transmit files using the SFTP protocol, and the AWS Transfer Family stores them as S3 objects in the landing zone in the data lake.

## Amazon AppFlow

The AppFlow service enables SAAS applications to ingest data into the data lake.

# Data Storage Services

Storing data seamlessly is one of the most crucial aspects of a well-built data platform. You need to build a data lake, which is nothing but data stored in a raw/unprocessed manner, which will act as a data repository. Now let's take a look at how Amazon S3 will help us to achieve this.

## Data Lake Implementation Through Amazon S3

When it comes to a data lake service in a serverless data platform, we can unanimously choose Amazon S3 as it provides unlimited scaling, intelligent tiering of data, availability of 99.99 percent, and durability of 99.999999999 percent, which makes it an ideal candidate for data lake implementation in a data platform.

Data of any format can be stored in S3 buckets without any predefined schema. After ingesting data into the S3 data lake, the processing layer can define the schema on top of Amazon S3 datasets and then use it to apply the required structure to the data obtained from the S3 objects.

The AWS Lake Formation service from AWS can be used in conjunction with S3 to build data lakes. The AWS Lake Formation service helps to build, secure, and manage data lakes easily in a few simple steps.

## Data Processing Services

The processing layer mainly consists of services that can be used to perform the extraction, transformation, and loading of data (aka ETL processes). Most of the ETL services in AWS are now available as serverless services as well. Let's take a look at them.

## AWS Glue

AWS Glue is a serverless ETL service that is built on top of Apache Spark and provides commonly used data source connectors, structures, and ETL transformations to validate, clean, transform, and flatten data stored in many open-source formats such as CSV, JSON, Parquet, etc.

We can also use Glue crawlers to populate the AWS Glue data catalog with tables. We can define and run crawlers that can crawl multiple data stores and upon completion create a table in the data catalog that can be used as a source for the ETL jobs. Figure 5-4 shows a sample Glue job to catalog data from an S3 data lake.

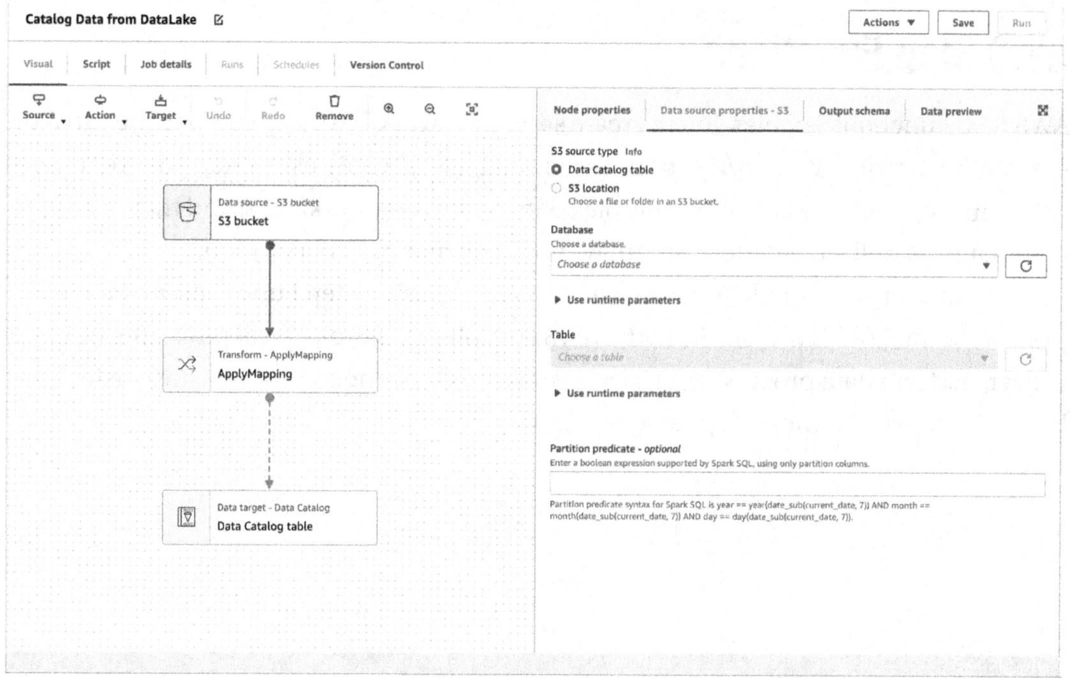


***Figure 5-4.*** *A Glue job in AWS*

## Amazon EMR (Serverless)

Amazon EMR is a platform service from AWS that helps run Big Data frameworks such as Apache Hadoop and Apache Spark. Amazon EMR Serverless is a new option in Amazon EMR that enables its users to run EMR without having to manage EMR clusters as the compute is fully managed from AWS. If we need to harness Spark or Hadoop for data processing and we need the serverless option as well, then we can use the EMR Serverless feature.

## Amazon Athena

Amazon Athena is a serverless interactive query service that can be used to query data in S3. Since we are using S3 as the data lake, we can use Athena to prepare data for analysis. As Athena integrates with the AWS Glue data catalog, it helps to populate the Lake Formation catalog with new and modified table and partition definitions, and it maintains schema versioning.

## AWS Step Functions

AWS Step Functions enables you to create serverless workflows that can be scheduled or event-driven using AWS services such as Lambda, ECS, etc. By using Step Functions and AWS Glue together, we can build complex data processing workflows, and they can be automated as well so that they can run without any manual intervention.

Let's look at an example to create an EMR cluster using Step Functions, using the project "Manage an EMR job" from the AWS console. This project will provision an EMR cluster, perform data processing in a couple of steps, and then terminate the cluster. Figure 5-5 illustrates these steps at a high level.

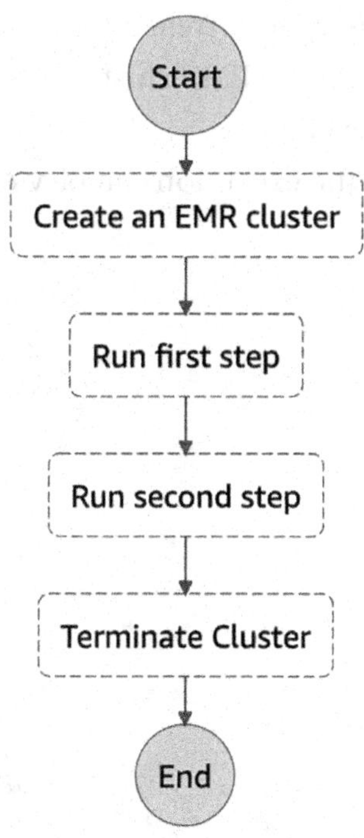


***Figure 5-5.*** *EMR cluster creation steps through the Step Functions service*

Once we execute this project, we can visualize the entire flow, as shown in Figure 5-6.

***Figure 5-6.*** *Step Functions flow visualization*

We can click each step and view the corresponding details related to each step. In Figure 5-5, I have clicked the "Create an EMR cluster" step, and its corresponding task input, parameters, etc., are displayed.

The events corresponding to the execution can be viewed as well on the same page, as shown in Figure 5-7.

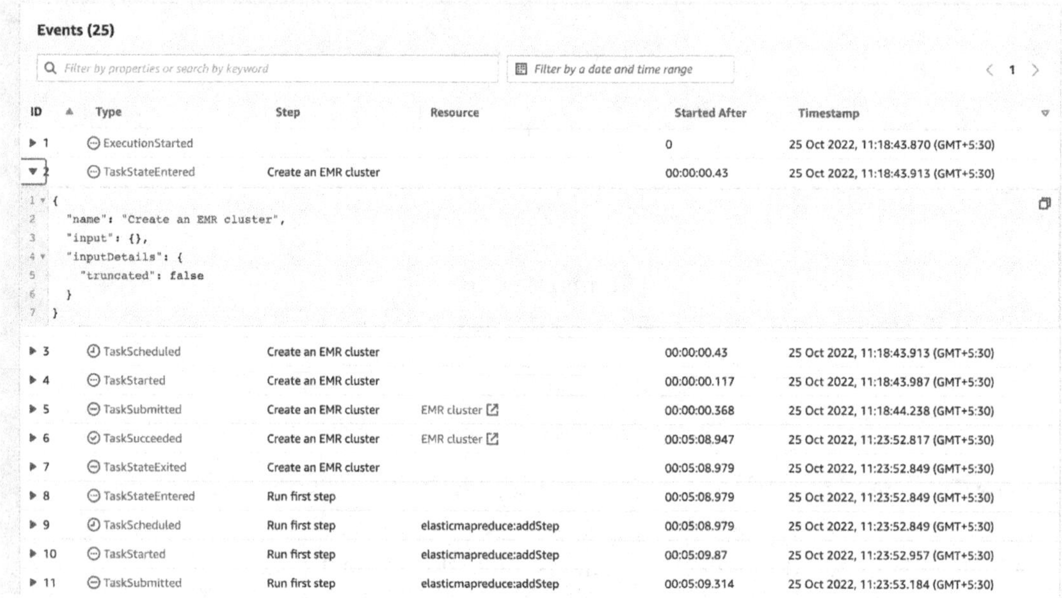

**Events (25)**

Filter by properties or search by keyword | Filter by a date and time range | < 1 >

| ID | Type | Step | Resource | Started After | Timestamp |
|---|---|---|---|---|---|
| 1 | ExecutionStarted | | | 0 | 25 Oct 2022, 11:18:43.870 (GMT+5:30) |
| 2 | TaskStateEntered | Create an EMR cluster | | 00:00:00.43 | 25 Oct 2022, 11:18:43.913 (GMT+5:30) |


```
{
  "name": "Create an EMR cluster",
  "input": {},
  "inputDetails": {
    "truncated": false
  }
}
```


| ID | Type | Step | Resource | Started After | Timestamp |
|---|---|---|---|---|---|
| 3 | TaskScheduled | Create an EMR cluster | | 00:00:00.43 | 25 Oct 2022, 11:18:43.913 (GMT+5:30) |
| 4 | TaskStarted | Create an EMR cluster | | 00:00:00.117 | 25 Oct 2022, 11:18:43.987 (GMT+5:30) |
| 5 | TaskSubmitted | Create an EMR cluster | EMR cluster | 00:00:00.368 | 25 Oct 2022, 11:18:44.238 (GMT+5:30) |
| 6 | TaskSucceeded | Create an EMR cluster | EMR cluster | 00:05:08.947 | 25 Oct 2022, 11:23:52.817 (GMT+5:30) |
| 7 | TaskStateExited | Create an EMR cluster | | 00:05:08.979 | 25 Oct 2022, 11:23:52.849 (GMT+5:30) |
| 8 | TaskStateEntered | Run first step | | 00:05:08.979 | 25 Oct 2022, 11:23:52.849 (GMT+5:30) |
| 9 | TaskScheduled | Run first step | elasticmapreduce:addStep | 00:05:08.979 | 25 Oct 2022, 11:23:52.849 (GMT+5:30) |
| 10 | TaskStarted | Run first step | elasticmapreduce:addStep | 00:05:09.87 | 25 Oct 2022, 11:23:52.957 (GMT+5:30) |
| 11 | TaskSubmitted | Run first step | elasticmapreduce:addStep | 00:05:09.314 | 25 Oct 2022, 11:23:53.184 (GMT+5:30) |

***Figure 5-7.*** *Events corresponding to EMR cluster creation*

Now, let's explore how data is consumed and visualized using AWS services.

# Data Consumption and Visualization Services

Data consumption and visualization services mainly include querying services, BI tools, and visualization dashboards.

# Amazon Athena

As mentioned in the "Data Processing Services" section, Athena is used for interactive querying. Using Athena, we can run complex ANSI queries against datasets without having to load them to a staging database, and we are charged only for the queries we run.

# Amazon Redshift

Redshift is Amazon's data warehousing solution that can process petabytes of data and run thousands of highly performant queries in parallel. Redshift Serverless is the serverless offering of Amazon Redshift that provisions data warehouse capacity and scales dynamically. Figure 5-8 shows the serverless dashboard for Amazon Redshift, and Figure 5-9 shows the Query Editor where we can load data and start querying directly.

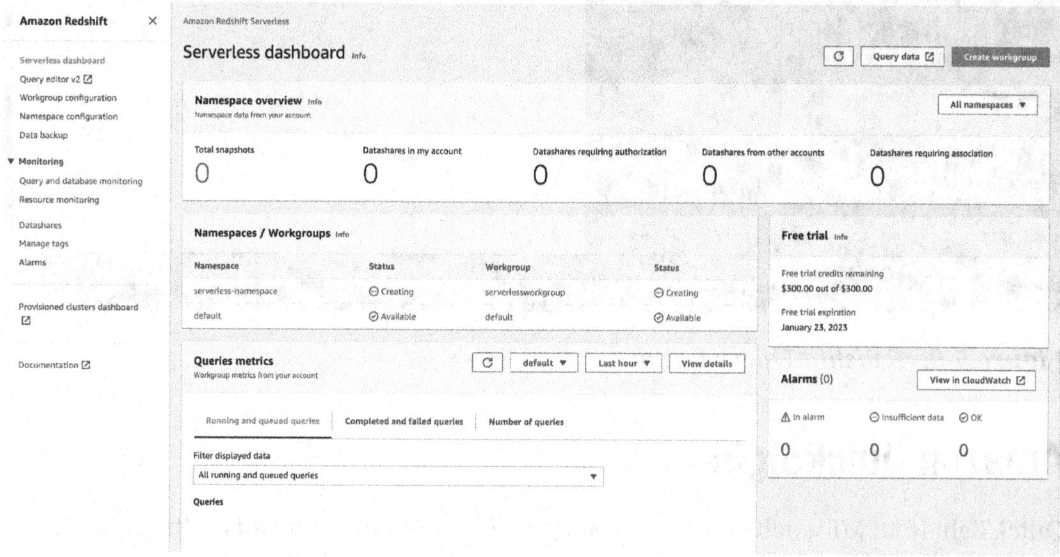


*Figure 5-8.* *Redshift Serverless dashboard*

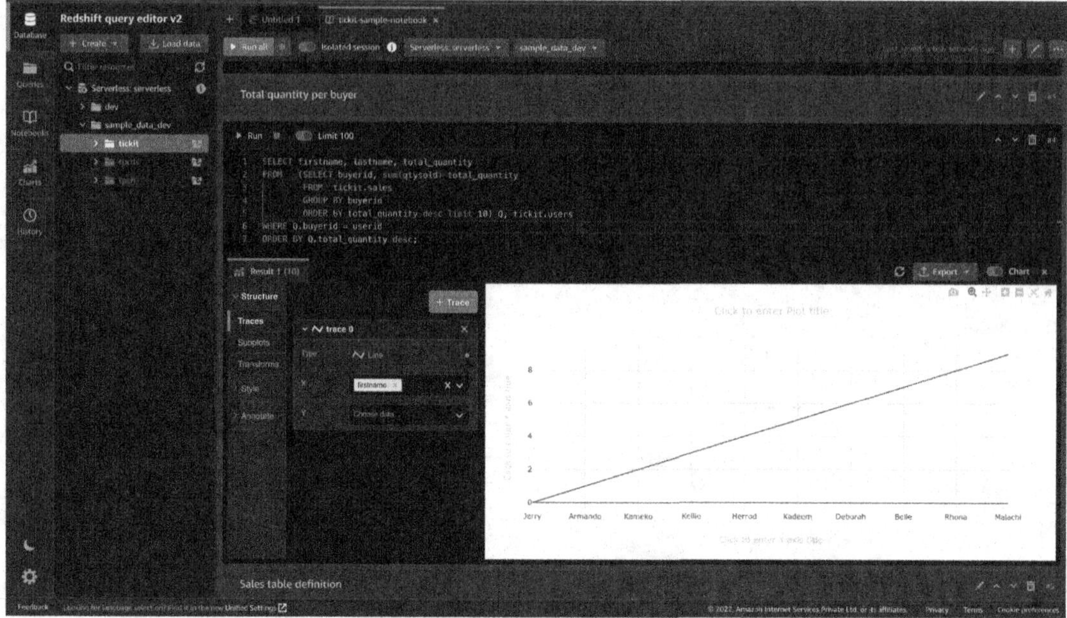


***Figure 5-9.*** *Redshift Query Editor*

# Amazon QuickSight

QuickSight is an ML-enabled BI tool that is used for visualization and for the creation of interactive dashboards. QuickSight implements ML insights such as forecasting, anomaly detection, and narrative dashboards.

As per the AWS documentation, QuickSight allows you to connect and import data from the following:

- SaaS applications, such as Salesforce, Square, ServiceNow, Twitter, GitHub, and JIRA
- Third-party databases, such as Teradata, MySQL, Postgres, and SQL Server
- Native AWS services, such as Amazon Redshift, Athena, Amazon S3, and Amazon Relational Database Service (Amazon RDS)
- Private VPC subnets

It also supports the upload of the XLS, CSV, JSON, and Presto file types.

## Building a Serverless Data Analytics Application

Using the serverless services discussed previously, we can design a variety of data-centric applications. In this section, let's look at building a data analytics application using serverless services. Figure 5-10 shows the high-level architecture of this application.

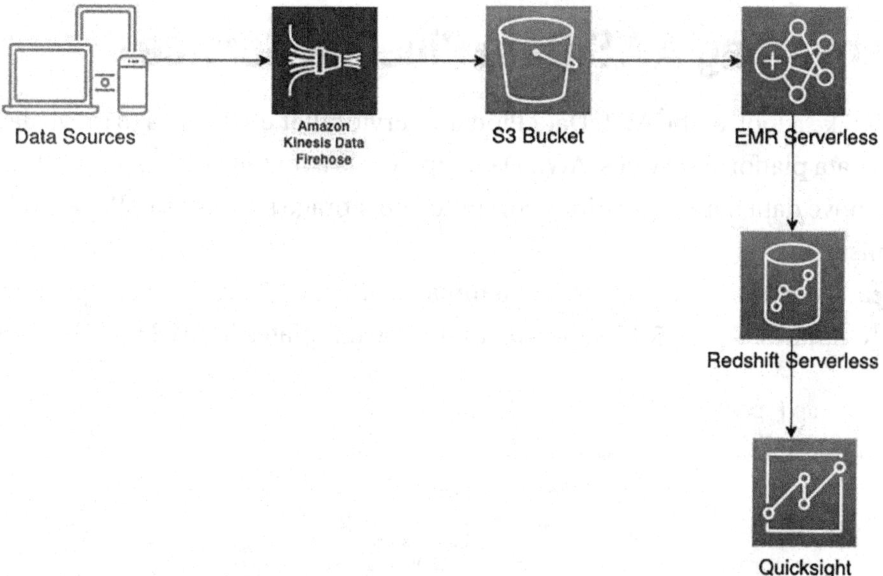


***Figure 5-10.*** *A serverless data analytics application*

Some of the main advantages of using serverless platform services to build an analytics application are the flexibility it brings in terms of cost, the simplicity in implementation, and managed scaling, which are essential for building a seamless data analytics application. Now, let's take a look at the architectural components and their role in this architecture:

- *Data ingestion*: We use Kinesis Data Firehose to ingest data from multiple sources into AWS S3.
- *Data storage*: We use S3 as a data lake for storing raw data.
- *Data processing*: We use EMR Serverless to sort, aggregate, and join datasets.

- *Data warehousing*: We use Amazon Redshift Serverless as the data warehousing solution. The transformed data is loaded into the Redshift database.
- *Data Visualization*: We use Amazon QuickSight to create interactive dashboards with the data from Redshift.

# Implementing AWS Data Pipeline Service

Now let's take a look at the AWS Data Pipeline service that enables us to move data between data platform services. AWS Data Pipeline is a managed ETL service that helps to move data between various compute and storage services in AWS as well as on-premise.

We can create workflows based on templates provided by AWS or using our own custom templates. Figure 5-11 shows ready-to-use templates in AWS Data Pipeline.

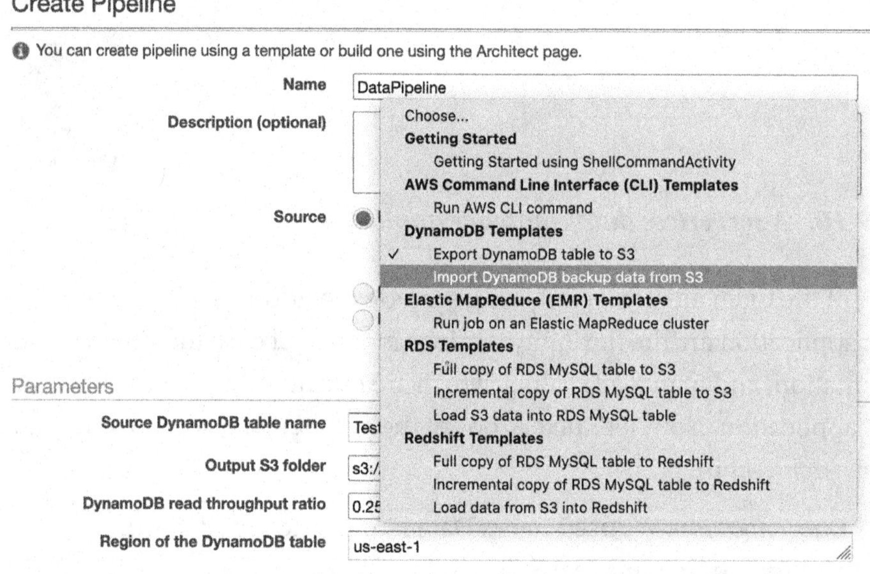


***Figure 5-11.*** *Templates to build a data platform*

Now let's build a pipeline that will import data from a DynamoDB table into an S3 bucket.

1. Fill in the name of the pipeline and set the source to "Build using a Template."
2. **Step 2:** Choose the DynamoDB template called Export DynamoDB Table to S3.
3. **Step 3:** Choose the DynamoDB source table, and set Output to the S3 folder.

We are importing data from a DynamoDB table called TestTable, as shown in Figure 5-12.

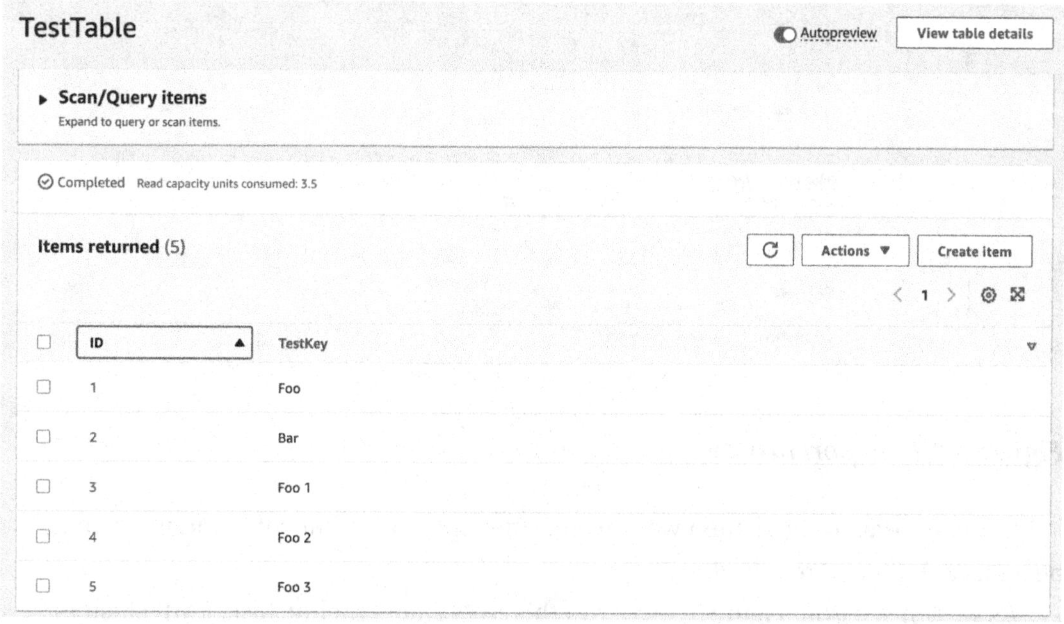


***Figure 5-12.** DynamoDB table for data export*

We are exporting this table to an S3 bucket, and the logs are persisted in the same bucket as well for ease of implementation.

4. Choose the roles for AWS Data Pipeline and for the EC2 instance role. This will give the data pipeline the necessary permissions to perform the actions on AWS resources.

Figure 5-13 shows this data populated in the respective fields.

Parameters

Source DynamoDB table name TestTable

Output S3 folder s3://datapipeline-import-testtable/imported-data/

DynamoDB read throughput ratio 0.25

Region of the DynamoDB table us-east-1

Schedule

You can run your pipeline once or specify a schedule. More

Run on pipeline activation

on a schedule

Run every 1 day(s)

Starting on pipeline activation

2022-10-25 17:31 UTC (Current time is 17:57 UTC)

YYYY-MM-DD HH:MM

Ending never

after 1 occurrence(s)

2022-10-26 17:31 UTC (Current time is 17:57 UTC)

YYYY-MM-DD HH:MM

Pipeline Configuration

Logging Enabled

Disabled

Copy execution logs to S3. More

S3 location for logs

s3://datapipeline-import-testtable/logs/

Security/Access

IAM roles IAM Roles let you control permissions for AWS Data Pipeline and your EC2 applications. More

Pipeline role DataePipelineRole

Control what AWS Data Pipeline can do with resources in your account. More

EC2 instance role EC2InstanceRole

Control what EC2 applications can do with resources in your account. More

***Figure 5-13.*** *Export task configurations*

Once this data is filled, then we can view the pipeline architecture and make the necessary changes if required.

As we can see from Figure 5-14, to run this AWS Data Pipeline task, EMR clusters are launched. Make sure that you set the "Terminate after" property to True so that the clusters get terminated after the pipeline execution is completed.

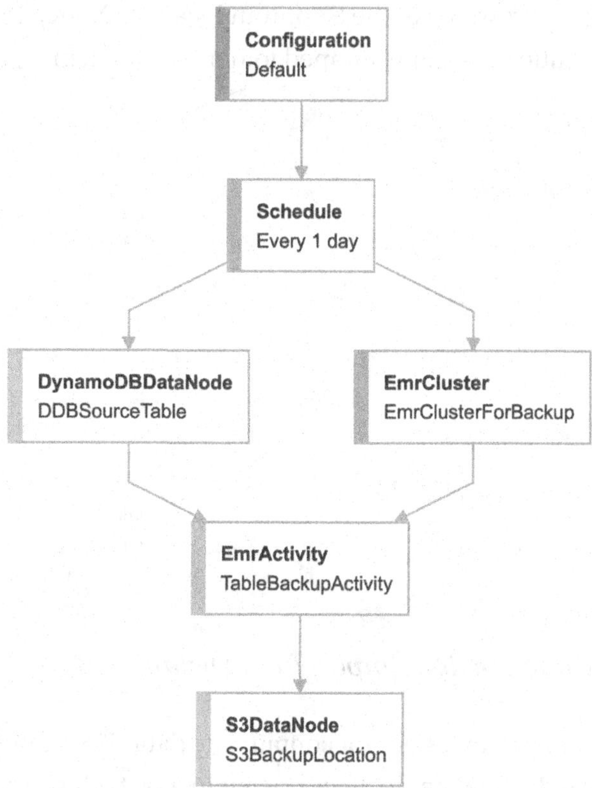


***Figure 5-14.*** *Data pipeline overview for DynamoDB export to S3*

Once you click Activate, the pipeline gets created, and on the Data Pipeline dashboard we can see the status of the pipeline along with the execution details, as shown in Figure 5-15.

Data Pipeline List Pipelines DataPipeline Help

Create new pipeline Actions

Filter: All Filter pipelines ... 2 pipelines (all loaded)

| Pipeline ID | Name | Schedule State | Health Status | Creation Time (UTC) |
|---|---|---|---|---|
| df-042117010PSOC966YKJM | DataPipeline | SCHEDULED Runs every 1 day | HEALTHY | 2022-10-25 18:02:27 |

Schedule information
Start 2022-10-25 18:03:22 (UTC)
Period Runs every 1 day
Tags
— View all / Edit
Edit pipeline

| Activity | Type | Health Status | Last Completed Run (UTC) | Active Run (UTC) | Next Run (UTC) |
|---|---|---|---|---|---|
| TableBackupActivity | EmrActivity | HEALTHY | 2022-10-25 18:03:22 | - | 2022-10-26 18:03:22 |

View execution details

***Figure 5-15.*** *Data pipeline dashboard*

We can verify this by browsing to the S3 output location. Notice that three files have been created in the location in a timestamped folder, as shown in Figure 5-16.

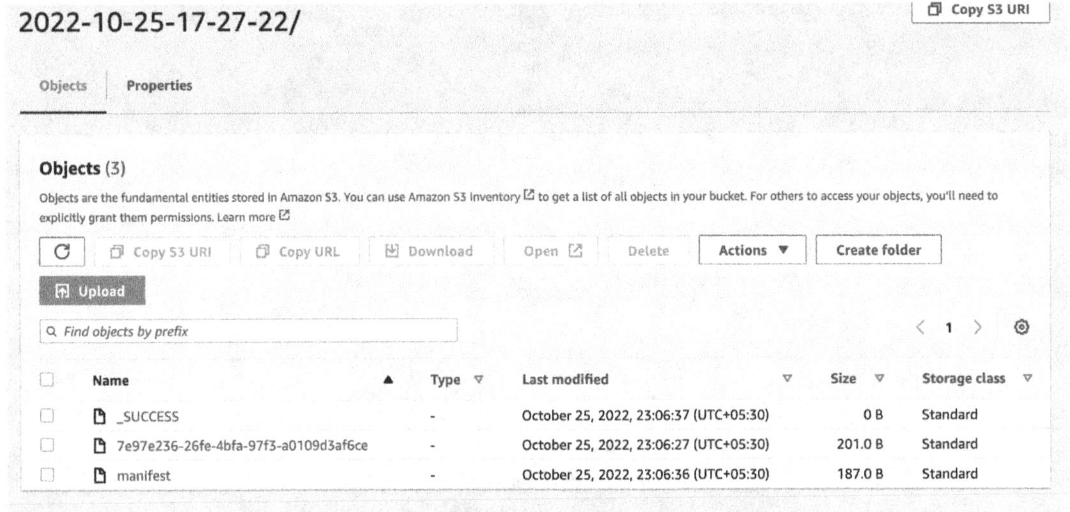


***Figure 5-16.*** *Verification of data import from DynamoDB*

The success and manifest files do not contain any data. The imported data is found in the file with the hexadecimal name. If we open it in a text editor, we can verify the data imported from DynamoDB. See Figure 5-17.

```
{"TestKey":{"s":"Bar"},"ID":{"s":"2"}}
{"TestKey":{"s":"Foo"},"ID":{"s":"1"}}
{"TestKey":{"s":"Foo 3"},"ID":{"s":"5"}}
{"TestKey":{"s":"Foo 2"},"ID":{"s":"4"}}
{"TestKey":{"s":"Foo 1"},"ID":{"s":"3"}}
```

***Figure 5-17.*** *Data imported from DynamoDB placed in an S3 file*

Thus, we learned how to use AWS Data Pipeline to transfer data between DynamoDB and S3. AWS Data Pipeline can be used for various other data transfer use cases as well. It really comes in handy when we need to orchestrate a workflow quickly, as a data pipeline can be set up in a few minutes.

# Conclusion

In this chapter, you got an overview of data platforms, saw the advantages of running a data platform on the cloud, explored the serverless services that can be used to construct the data platform layers, saw how to build a data analytics application on serverless, and utilized a completely managed data pipeline service.

The services are always evolving, so stay updated on the latest features. In the next chapter, we will see how we can leverage the power of containers on a serverless platform.

# CHAPTER 6

# Containers on Serverless

You likely have some familiarity with containers and the immense capabilities they add to the infrastructure world. Nowadays, containers are ubiquitous, and hence it is vital to understand how they operate in the cloud and, more specifically, AWS. This chapter gives you insight into how you can use serverless container services to design applications.

Over the course of this chapter, we will cover the following topics:

- Overview of containers
- AWS ecosystem for containers
- Running container-based workloads on serverless
- Serverless architectures using containers

## Overview of Containers

A *container* is a software package that contains all the dependencies to run an application in a computing environment. Containers, unlike virtual machines, do not provide virtualization at a hardware level but at an operating system level.

To run a container, you need to have a container runtime that is installed on a host machine. To run an application on this container, you can use a base image of your application, which contains the necessary dependencies.

Figure 6-1 shows the differences in architecture with respect to virtual machines and containers.




J. J. Paul, *Distributed Serverless Architectures on AWS*, https://doi.org/10.1007/978-1-4842-9159-7_6

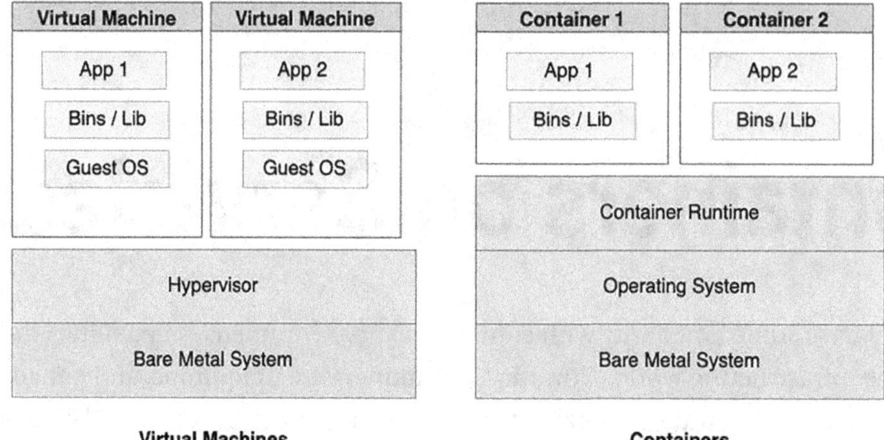


***Figure 6-1.*** *Virtual machines versus containers*

As you can see from Figure 6-1, the container runtime harnesses the underlying operating system to run all containers, whereas for virtual machines, each virtual machine has a different operating system.

Now let's take a look at the different serverless services available on AWS for containers.

## Serverless Container Services on AWS

There are a number of services on AWS that will help when running containers on AWS. In this section, we will focus on the serverless container services on AWS, as illustrated in Figure 6-2.

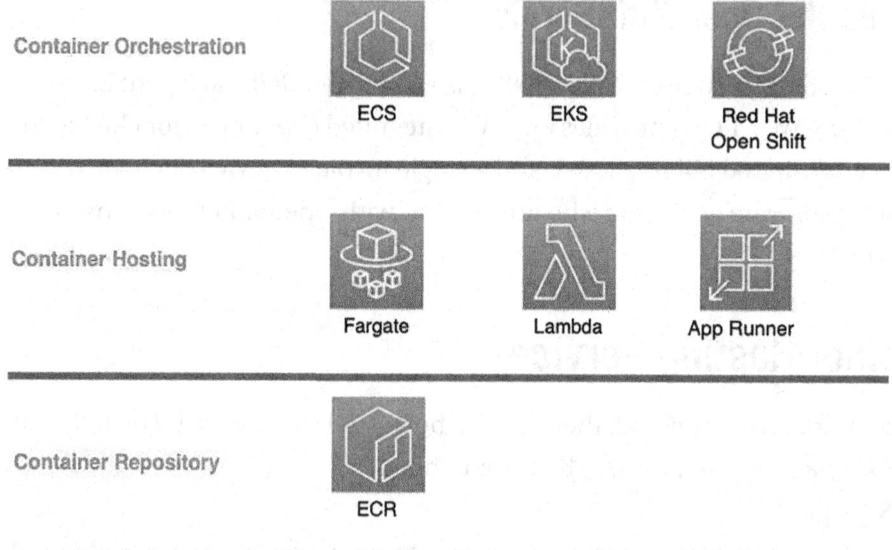


***Figure 6-2.*** *AWS serverless ecosystem for containers*

# Container Orchestration Services

While running containers on any platform, be it cloud or on-premises, it is essential that there is a container orchestration service to orchestrate the fleet of containers, which in essence involves managing the containers from end to end. In this section, we look at the container orchestration services available on AWS.

## AWS Elastic Container Service (ECS)

ECS is the AWS container orchestration platform. It is a fully managed service that can be used to deploy, scale, and manage containers. ECS also supports a wide variety of compute options such as Fargate, Outposts, AWS Local Zone, etc.

## AWS Elastic Kubernetes Service (EKS)

EKS is the managed Kubernetes service from AWS. You can run Kubernetes workloads on the AWS cloud or on-premises using EKS. EKS manages the control plane nodes, and we need to take care of the worker nodes, which can be deployed into EC2 worker nodes or Fargate-based serverless nodes.

## AWS Red Hat OpenShift Service

Red Hat OpenShift Service on AWS (ROSA) is a managed Red Hat OpenShift integration on AWS. ROSA provides an AWS-integrated experience for cluster creation, a consumption-based billing model, and a single invoice for AWS deployments. It also enables software engineers who are familiar with OpenShift tools to extend their platform to AWS.

# Container Hosting Services

To run containers on the cloud, they need to be hosted in the cloud. The following are the AWS services we can utilize to host containers:

**AWS Fargate**

When it comes to using a serverless compute engine for hosting containers, AWS Fargate is the most suitable choice. Fargate is a fully managed compute infrastructure platform that takes care of the scaling, managing, and securing of servers.

**AWS Lambda**

AWS Lambda supports container images as a deployment package. We can use an AWS-provided base image or an Alpine or Debian image. However, there are a few prerequisites to be met to use container images as Lambda deployment packages. We will learn more about that later in this chapter.

**AWS AppRunner**

AWS AppRunner is a fully managed service that enables developers to deploy containerized applications easily without any infrastructure management overhead. The only configurations required are the CPU and memory required for the container and the autoscaling configuration.

# Container Registry Service

The container registry service is used as a repository to store images from which a container can be spun up. In AWS, the container registry service is ECR, which is explained next.

**Elastic Container Registry (ECR)**

ECR is a fully managed container image repository where we can push images directly without having to provision any infrastructure. You can store both public and private images as well in ECR. It can be accessed via the console, an SDK, or the CLI.

## Container Modernization

Container modernization involves the steps needed to modernize a stand-alone application workload into a container-based workload. In AWS, we have the App2Container service to achieve this.

**AWS App2Container**

AWS App2Container is a command-line utility from AWS that helps to containerize .NET and Java applications running on virtual machines, EC2 instances, or bare metal. If we select the required applications to modernize, the App2Container tool will package the application artifacts and dependencies into container images, add the required configurations, and generate the necessary Amazon ECS and Amazon EKS deployment artifacts.

## Serverless Web Application Architecture Using Fargate

Now that we have familiarized ourselves with serverless services for containers, let's take a look at a use case. Figure 6-3 shows the architecture for a serverless web application using the Fargate compute platform.

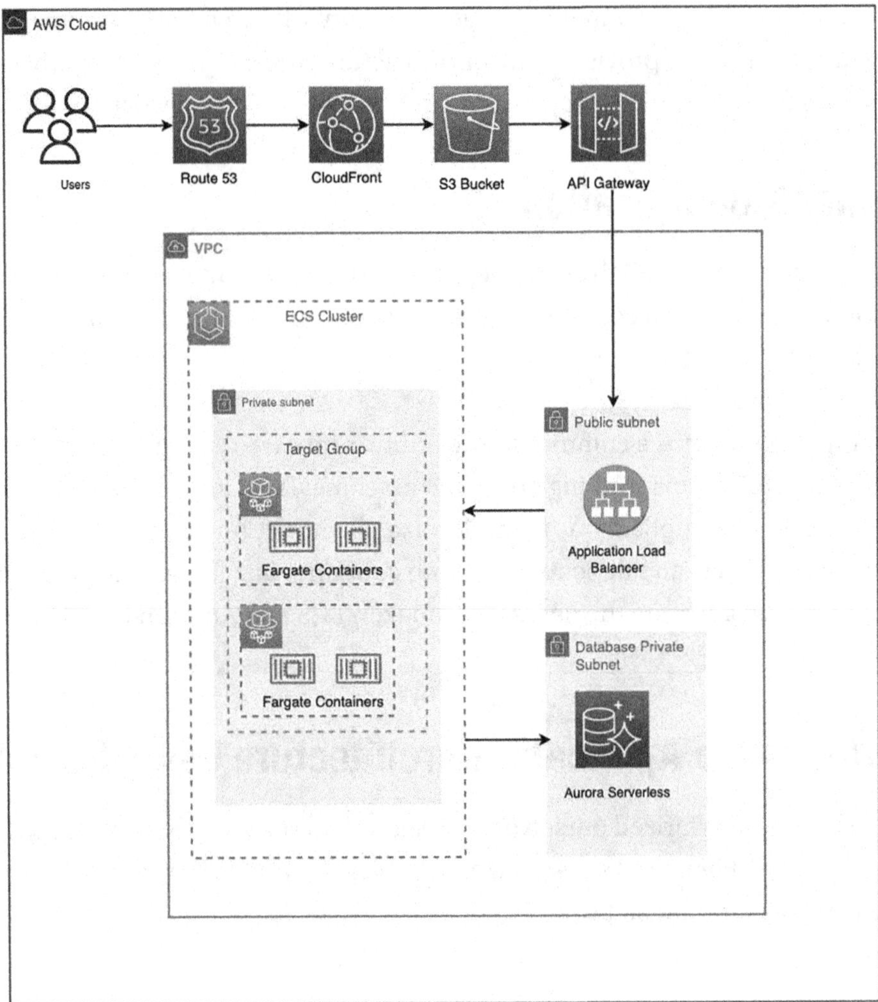


***Figure 6-3.*** *A serverless web application using Fargate*

The front end is hosted using S3, and it is delivered using CloudFront. The APIs are hosted in Fargate containers, which sit behind an application load balancer. The API Gateway integrates to the application load balancer, which distributes the traffic between the containers.

Now, let's look at how we can deploy containers into Fargate and use ECS for its orchestration. But before that, let's get familiar with Fargate components.

- *Cluster*: A cluster is a logical grouping of tasks and services. You define the subnets across which your cluster will run; also, it gives you the option to add additional compute capacity on top of Fargate like EC2 and ECS anywhere. Figure 6-4 shows the cluster dashboard.

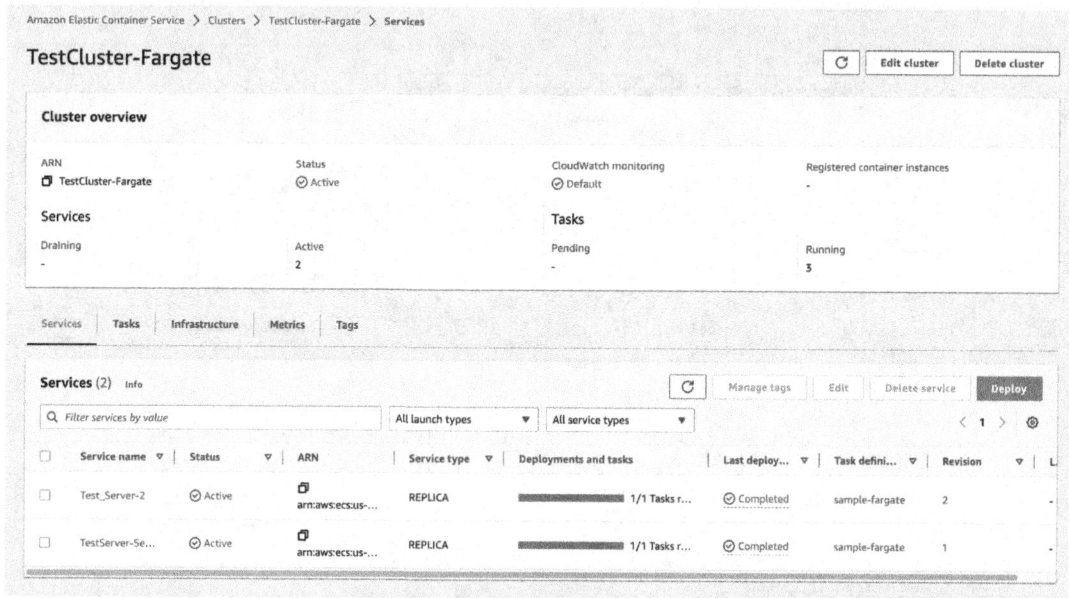


***Figure 6-4.*** *Fargate cluster dashboard*

- *Task definition*: A task definition is used to describe the containers that constitute your application. You can define a maximum of 10 containers using the task definition. You can also define the container port mapping, CPU, memory, etc., using the task definition. Figure 6-5 shows the task definition step using the console.

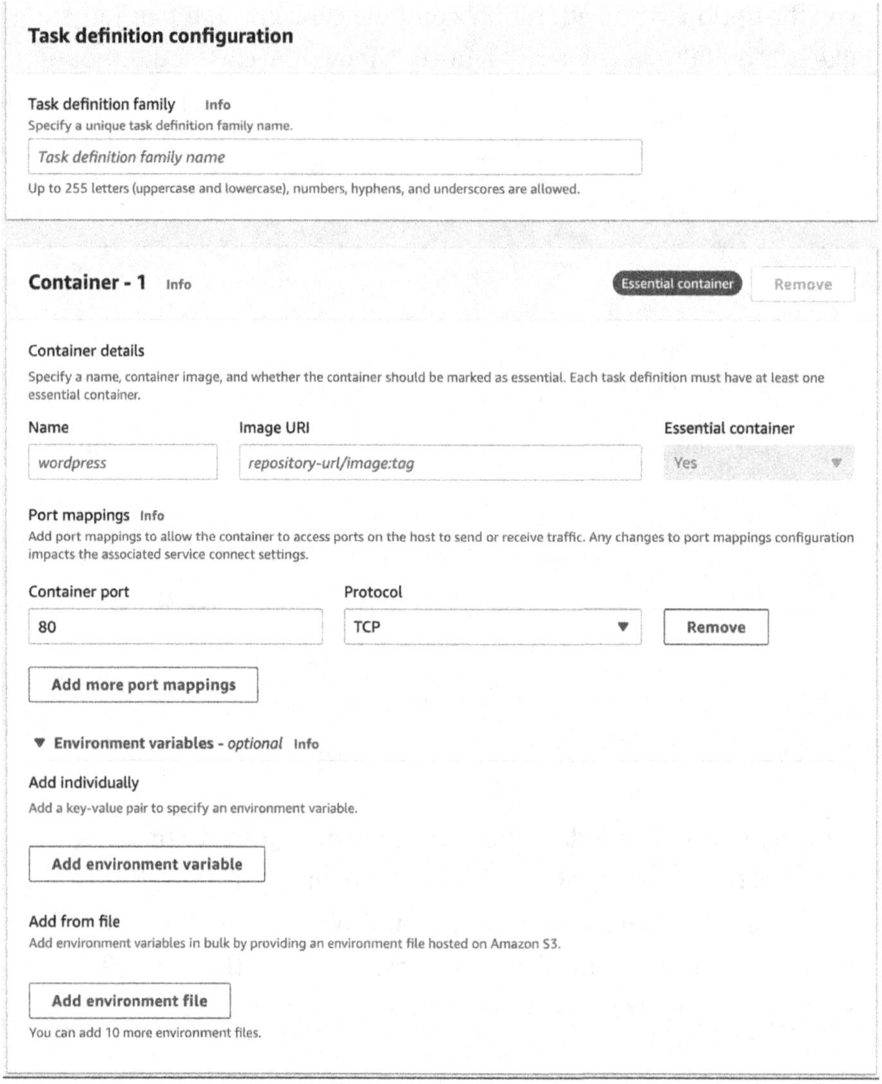

***Figure 6-5.** Configuring the task definition*

- *Tasks*: A task is an instantiation of the task definition. We can define the total number of tasks that need to run as part of the service or within a cluster.
- *Service*: A service represents a collection of tasks. A service can be used to manage tasks; i.e., if a task stops running, a service can replace the particular task with a new one based on the task definition.

# Running Containers using Serverless Services on AWS

Now that we have familiarized ourselves with the serverless container services on AWS, let's take a look at the implementation side of things and see how we can run containers on serverless services.

## Running Containers on Fargate

We can run containers on Fargate in a serverless flavor using both EKS and ECS services. Here we are considering ECS as the container orchestration service.

**Step 1: Create the ECS Cluster**

Specify the VPC and subnets where the cluster will be launched. Additionally, you can enable container insights, which will send all the metrics such as CPU utilization, memory, etc., into CloudWatch. Figure 6-6 illustrates these steps.

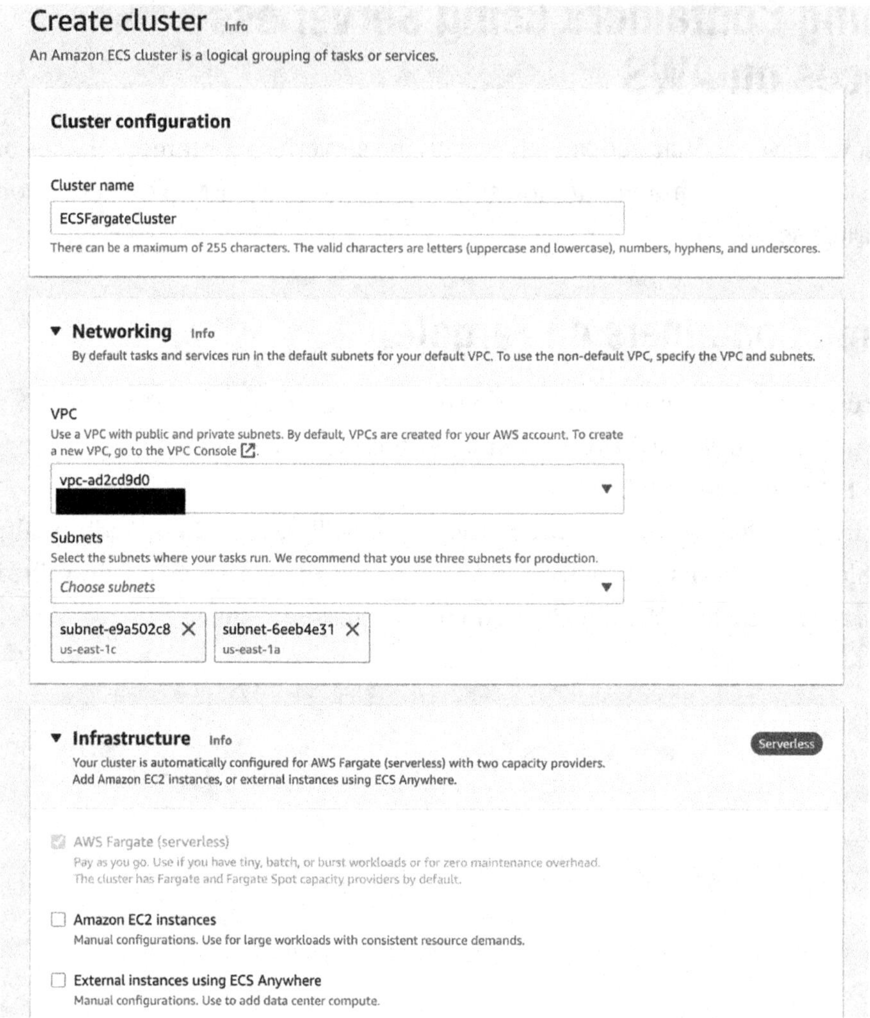

***Figure 6-6.*** *Creating a cluster*

### Step 2: Create the Task Definition

We can use the task definition JSON given next to create a task definition. The following JSON creates a simple HTTPD server by pulling a public Docker image from ECR:

```
{
    "family": "webapp-fargate",
    "networkMode": "awsvpc",
    "containerDefinitions": [
```

```
        {
            "name": "fargate-web-app",
            "image": "public.ecr.aws/docker/library/httpd:latest",
            "portMappings": [
                {
                    "containerPort": 80,
                    "hostPort": 80,
                    "protocol": "tcp"
                }
            ],
            "essential": true,
            "entryPoint": [
                "sh",
                "-c"
            ],
          "command": [
                "/bin/sh -c \"echo '<html> <head> <title>Welcome to
                Serverless Architectures </title> <style>body {margin-top:
                40px; background-color: #333;} </style> </head>
                </html>' >  /usr/local/apache2/htdocs/index.html &&
                httpd-foreground\""
            ]
        }
    ],
    "requiresCompatibilities": [
        "FARGATE"
    ],
    "cpu": "256",
    "memory": "512"
}
```

**Step 3: Deploy a Service with Tasks**

Now we can deploy a service that will run the tasks we create out of the task definition. The configurations are quite straightforward, as shown in Figure 6-7. I have chosen a rolling update here; feel free to choose other deployment options as well.

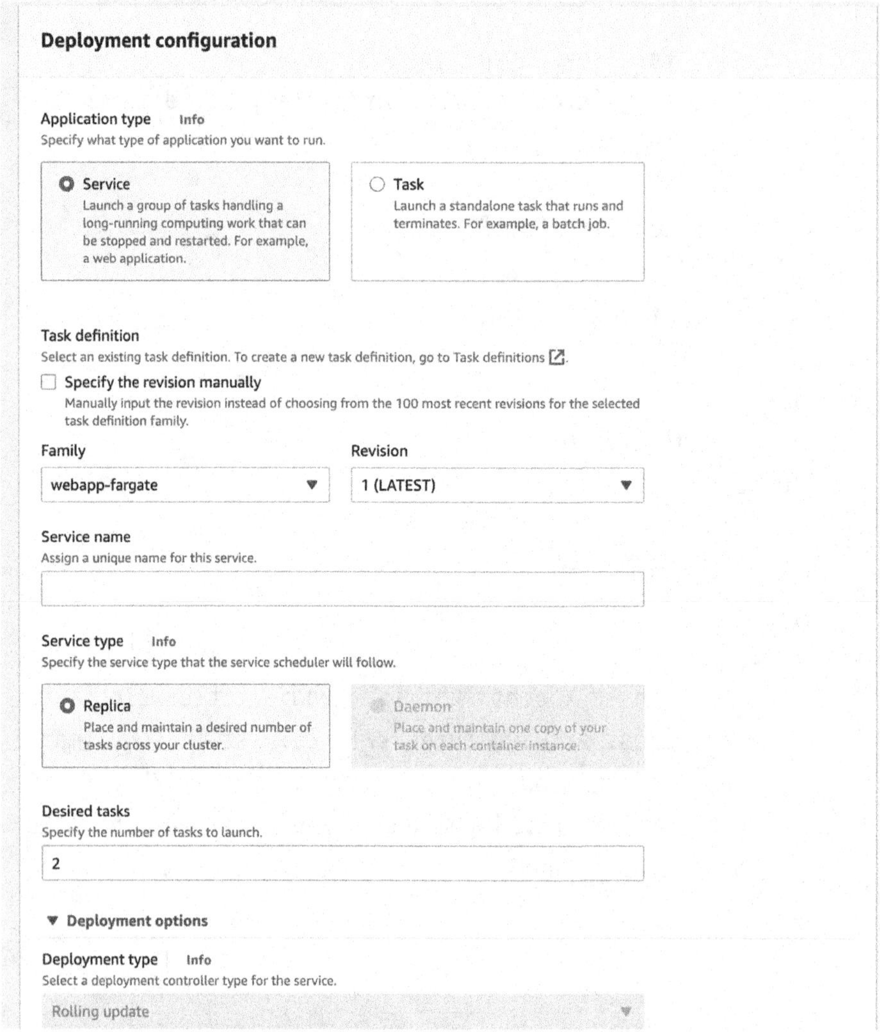

**Deployment configuration**

Application type Info
Specify what type of application you want to run.

Service
Launch a group of tasks handling a long-running computing work that can be stopped and restarted. For example, a web application.

Task
Launch a standalone task that runs and terminates. For example, a batch job.

Task definition
Select an existing task definition. To create a new task definition, go to Task definitions.

Specify the revision manually
Manually input the revision instead of choosing from the 100 most recent revisions for the selected task definition family.

Family
webapp-fargate

Revision
1 (LATEST)

Service name
Assign a unique name for this service.

Service type Info
Specify the service type that the service scheduler will follow.

Replica
Place and maintain a desired number of tasks across your cluster.

Daemon
Place and maintain one copy of your task on each container instance.

Desired tasks
Specify the number of tasks to launch.
2

▼ Deployment options

Deployment type Info
Select a deployment controller type for the service.
Rolling update

***Figure 6-7.*** *Service deployment*

For load balancing, we can use either application or network load balancers. For scaling, we can use service autoscaling, which manages the desired state of the tasks from ECS itself, as shown in Figure 6-8.

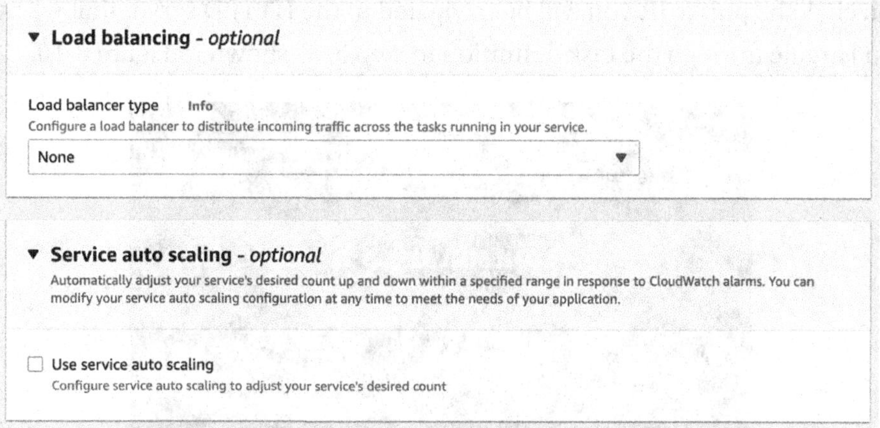

*Figure 6-8. Load balancing configuration*

### Step 4: Verify That the Tasks Are Running

Once your Fargate tasks are running, you can view their status by clicking the service name under the cluster, which is ECSFargateCluster, as shown in Figure 6-9. Clicking individual tasks will yield the public IP address of the container.

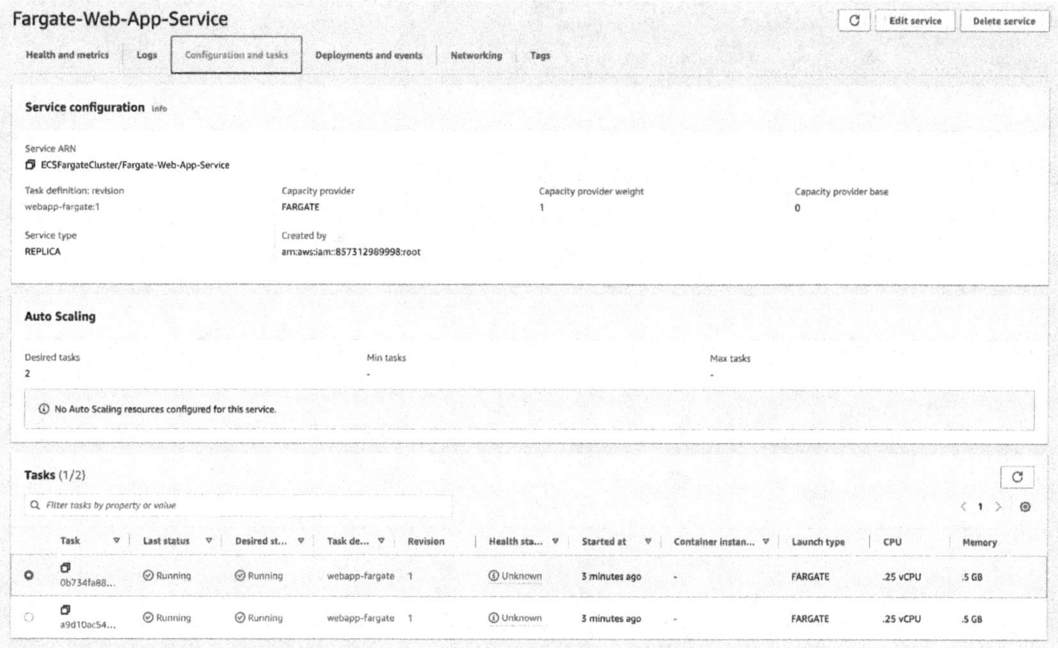

*Figure 6-9. Task status*

If you click the public IP, you will be navigated to the HTTPD server that we have hosted in Fargate through the task definition in step 2, as shown in Figure 6-10.

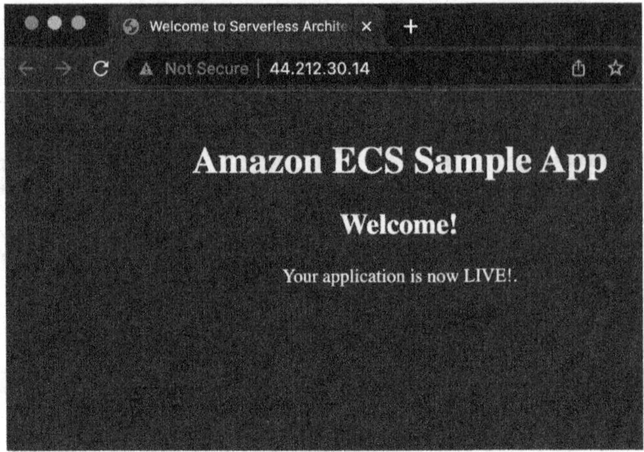


***Figure 6-10.*** *Browser output of the hosted app*

Additionally, we can create a revision of the task definition and deploy it (see Figure 6-11). The old tasks will be discontinued, and the new tasks will start running, as shown in Figure 6-12.

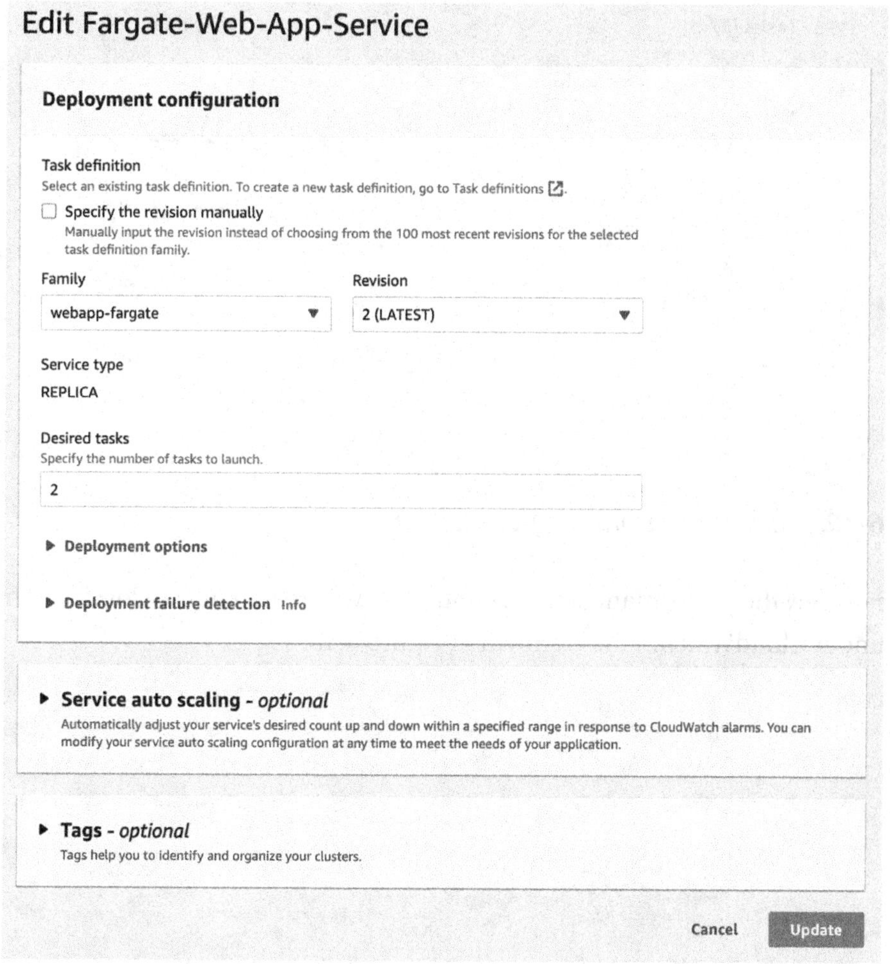

Edit Fargate-Web-App-Service

**Deployment configuration**

Task definition
Select an existing task definition. To create a new task definition, go to Task definitions.

Specify the revision manually
Manually input the revision instead of choosing from the 100 most recent revisions for the selected task definition family.

Family: webapp-fargate
Revision: 2 (LATEST)

Service type
REPLICA

Desired tasks
Specify the number of tasks to launch.
2

Deployment options

Deployment failure detection Info

**Service auto scaling** - *optional*
Automatically adjust your service's desired count up and down within a specified range in response to CloudWatch alarms. You can modify your service auto scaling configuration at any time to meet the needs of your application.

**Tags** - *optional*
Tags help you to identify and organize your clusters.

Cancel Update

***Figure 6-11.*** *Task revision option*

**Tasks** (1/4)

Filter tasks by property or value

| | Task | Last status | Desired st... | Task defin... |
|---|---|---|---|---|
| ● | 2872f84b4e... | Running | Running | webapp-fargate |
| ○ | 5f8e1b4174c... | Running | Running | webapp-fargate |
| ○ | 2beaae5ac27... | Stopped | Stopped | webapp-fargate |
| ○ | 997dd72eac... | Running | Stopped | webapp-fargate |

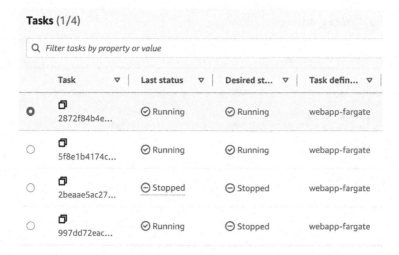

***Figure 6-12.** Task status update after revision*

We can view the performance of the containers we created in the Container Insights section under CloudWatch. This is shown in Figure 6-13.

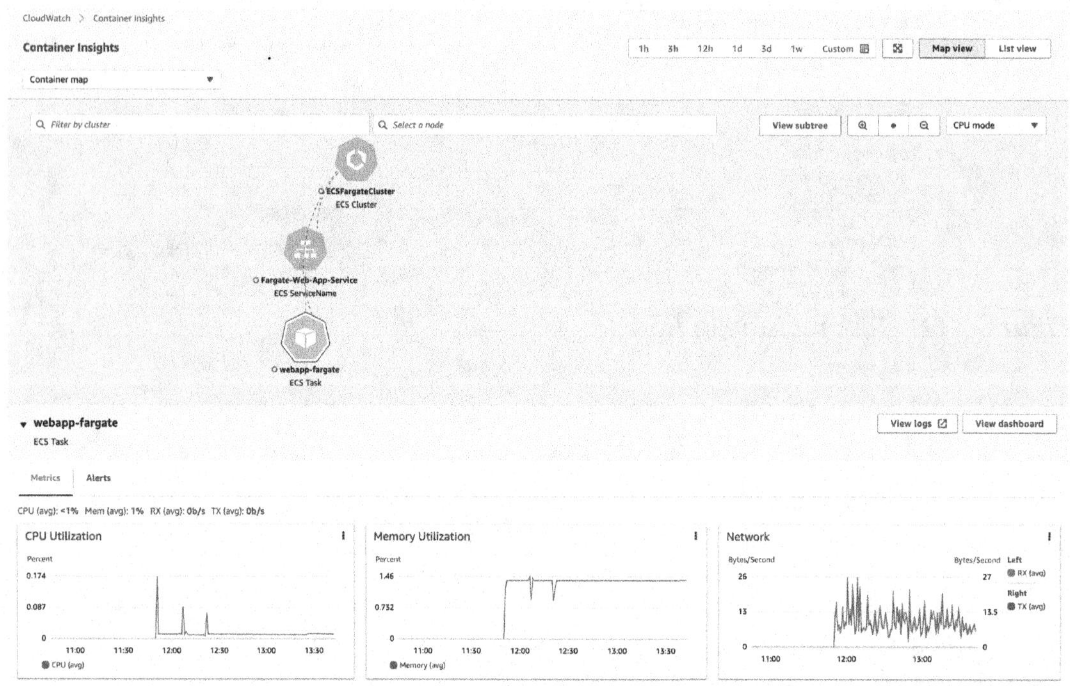


***Figure 6-13.** Container insights of the container we created*

## Running Containers on Lambda

To host container images on Lambda, there are a few prerequisites as per the AWS documentation.

- The AWS CLI and Docker CLIs are prerequisites to deploy any container image to Lambda.
- The Lambda Runtime API (`https://docs.aws.amazon.com/lambda/latest/dg/runtimes-api.html`) must be implemented by the container image.
- There must be a provision in the container image to be able to run on a read-only file system.
- The default user provided by Lambda is a Linux user with least-privileged permissions. This user must be able to read all the files that would be required to run the code.
- Only Linux-based images are currently supported by Lambda.
- Lambda supports only the functions that target a single architecture and do not support functions where multi-architecture container images are used.

We can follow the next steps to host a container on Lambda.

**Step1: Create or Add the Lambda Function**

Create a directory and add your Lambda function code there. I have used the code mentioned in the GitHub repo (`https://github.com/jithinjudepaule/Distributed_Serverless_Architectures_Book/tree/main/SampleApplications/SimpleWebApp`).

Kindly note that if you are using your own code, you must include a Lambda handler function and reference it in the Docker file.

```
// Lambda handler
exports.handler = function(event, context) {
  context.succeed("This is a sample web app hosted in lambda as container
  image");
};
```

**Step 2: Package the Lambda Function as an Image**

Include a Docker file to build an image out of the Lambda function. The contents of the Docker file are shown here:

```
FROM public.ecr.aws/lambda/nodejs:14
COPY SampleWebApp.js package*.json ./
RUN npm install
CMD [ "SampleWebApp.handler" ]
```

I have used a public Node.js image here. Kindly note I am pointing to my Lambda handler function so that Lambda recognizes the entry point for the function in the container image.

**Step 3: Build the Image**

Build the image using the following command from the Terminal:

```
docker build -t sample-webapp-container .
```

Note that you can always use a multistage Docker file to get the same output. I am following a step-by-step approach for simplicity.

You will get a similar output (for brevity, I have trimmed the output).

**Step 4: Log In to ECR Using the Terminal and Create a Repo**

Use the following command to log in to the ECR via Terminal:

```
aws ecr get-login-password  --region <region> | docker login
     --username AWS --password-stdin
    <accountID>.dkr.ecr.us-east-1.amazonaws.com
```

Note that the `get-login-password` command is used to retrieve an authentication token to authenticate to an Amazon ECR registry. Here we are retrieving the token and authenticating Docker to the ECR registry by passing the token to the Docker login command. We should also pass the ECR registry URI, which you want to authenticate to in the command

After you get the message "Login Succeeded," use the following command to create a repository:

```
aws ecr create-repository
     --repository-name <repositoryname>
     --image-tag-mutability IMMUTABLE
     --image-scanning-configuration scanOnPush=true
```

**Step 5: Tag and Push the Image**

Here's the command to tag the image:

```
docker tag <container name><account id>.dkr.ecr.<region>.amazonaws.
com/<repo name>:v1
```

Here's the command to push the image:

```
docker push <account id>.dkr.ecr.<region>.amazonaws.com/<repo name>:v1
```

After executing the previous commands, the image gets pushed to ECR, and we can verify this from the ECR console.

**Step 6: Create a Lambda Function with This Image**

Use the container image option from the Lambda function creation page and choose the image URI from the ECR repo, as shown in Figure 6-14.

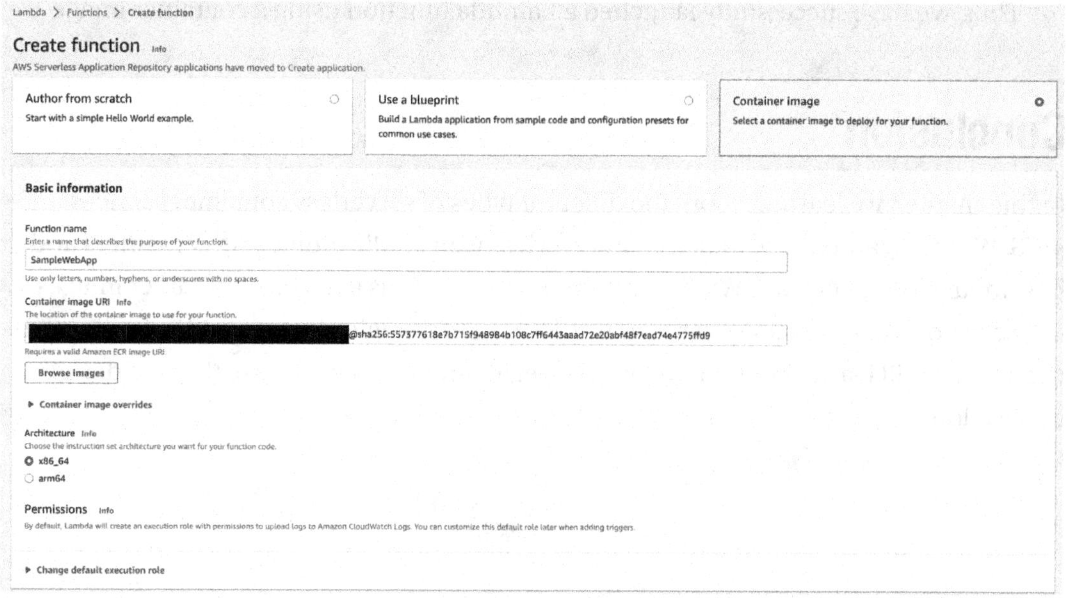

***Figure 6-14.*** *Choosing a container image to deploy the Lambda function*

**Step 7: Test the Lambda Function**

Test the created function by using a test event. We can see the results shown in Figure 6-15.

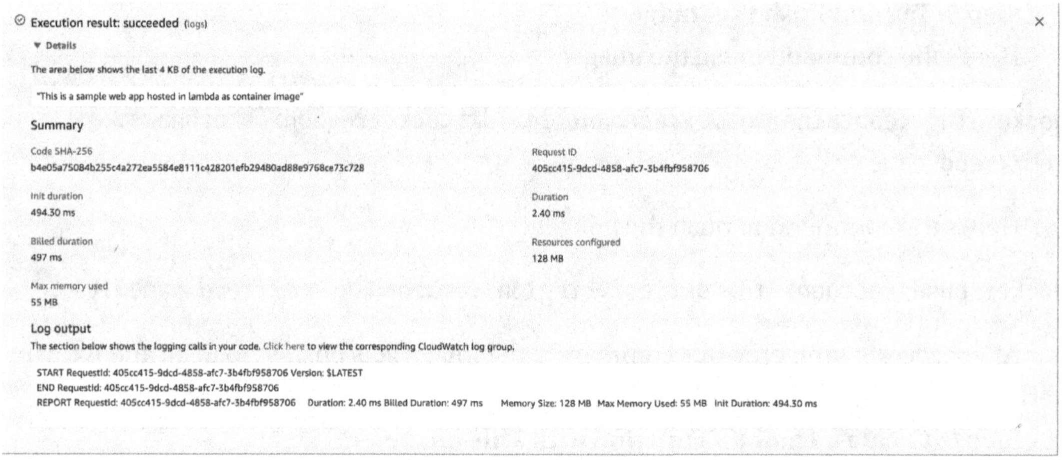

***Figure 6-15.*** *Testing the Lambda function created using the container image*

Thus, we have successfully launched a Lambda function using a container image.

# Conclusion

In this chapter, we learned about the different types of serverless container services on AWS. We also learned how to design a serverless web application using containers and how to run containers on AWS Fargate and use Lambda as a host for container images.

So far, our scope of cloud services was limited to a single cloud provider. In the next chapter, we will learn about multicloud strategies and how we can use them to design applications.

# CHAPTER 7

# Multicloud Architectures

The term *multicloud* signifies using multiple clouds for a single purpose. Nowadays enterprises want to harness the power of multiple clouds to run a single application so that they get maximum benefits from the application. This chapter discusses the following aspects of multicloud architectures:

- Types of cloud architectures
- Pros and cons of cloud architectures
- Multicloud architectures
- Comparison of multicloud architectures
- Real-world multicloud architectures

## Types of Cloud Architectures

There is no silver bullet for a perfect cloud architecture, and each comes with its pros and cons. Let's familiarize ourselves with the different types of cloud architecture.

## Single-Cloud Architecture

A single-cloud architecture is one of the most common implementations of cloud-based architectures where the entire application is hosted by a single cloud provider such as AWS, Azure, GCP, etc. Most enterprises that are embarking on their cloud journey get started with a single cloud as it is easy to get started and evaluate their workloads before triggering a full-blown migration to the cloud or greenfield cloud-native development. Figure 7-1 illustrates what a single-cloud application could look like. I have used the general cloud image to indicate that the single cloud could be any generic cloud, even a private cloud.




J. J. Paul, *Distributed Serverless Architectures on AWS*, https://doi.org/10.1007/978-1-4842-9159-7_7

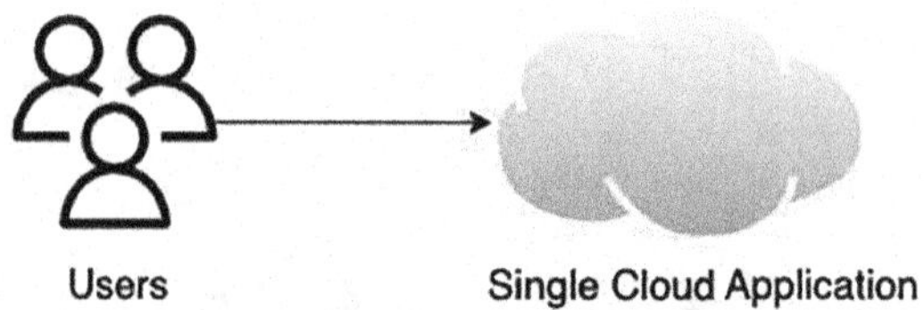


***Figure 7-1.*** *Single cloud architecture*

The following are the advantages of a single-cloud architecture:

- *Ease of management*: As all logs and trails can be grouped centrally, and it becomes easier to track issues.
- *Cost effective*: As all resources reside in a single cloud, a cost savings plan can be implemented across common resources such as virtual machines.
- *Ease of governance*: Account-level and group-level access control policies can be applied with ease.
- *Ease of testing*: It is easier to write integration tests as all components exist within the same environment.

These are the disadvantages of a single-cloud architecture:

- *Vendor lock-in*: Using services native to a single cloud will make it a difficult candidate for migration as the user will have to rewrite the application for a different cloud.
- *Risk of outage*: In the event of an outage at the cloud service provider level, our application will be unavailable as it relies on a single cloud provider.

## Hybrid Cloud Architecture

When organizations choose to keep part of their infrastructure in their local data centers and the remaining infrastructure in the cloud, the architecture is commonly known as a *hybrid* cloud architecture. Generally, enterprises choose this pattern as they can keep their critical data on-premises so that it is more secure and less vulnerable, and the less critical data can be hosted on the cloud. Organizations can use a VPN or a private network service such as AWS Direct Connect to connect to the cloud from on-premise systems. Figure 7-2 shows a hybrid cloud architecture on AWS. We are using the Direct Connect service to interconnect the on-premise data center with the AWS cloud.

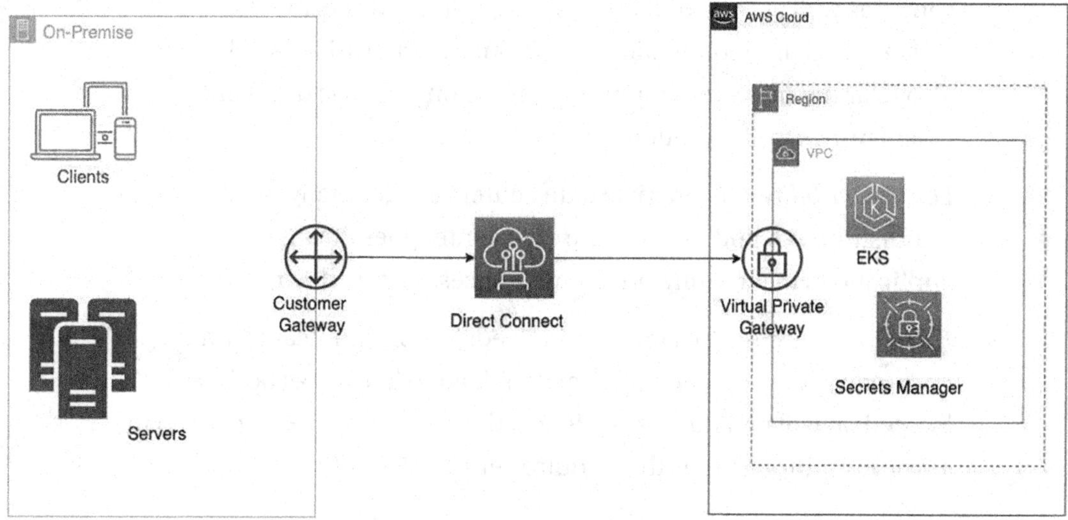


***Figure 7-2.** Hybrid cloud on AWS*

The following are the advantages of a hybrid cloud architecture:

- *Highly secure*: In a hybrid cloud, you can keep your critical data on-premises, which reduces the vulnerability attack vector.
- *More control*: In hybrid systems, if we feel that the cloud service provider is not allowing us to manage certain resources beyond a point, we can always host them on-premises and customize them in the way we want them to be.
- *Highly beneficial*: Depending on the use cases, enterprises can decide which features to implement in the public cloud and which features to implement on-premise. They can reap the benefits of scaling, availability, etc., from the public cloud and at the same time enjoy the benefits of using the internal application of the enterprise.

These are the disadvantages of a hybrid cloud architecture:

- *Expensive*: As enterprises need to spend on the on-premise data center as well as for cloud infrastructure, it will be costlier than a single-cloud implementation. Additionally, enterprises will have to also bear the management burden of the on-premise data centers, which brings forth additional costs.
- *Low availability*: On-premise data centers are generally nondistributed, and hence if the data center goes down, the applications that require on-premise access can go down as well.
- *Higher Latency*: As the application needs to communicate with the on-premise data center often, this can lead to latency as both are located on isolated networks. Hence, this becomes an anti-pattern for services or applications that require very low latency.

## Using AWS Outposts for Hybrid Cloud Solutions

AWS Outposts is a widely used service that helps organizations to implement hybrid cloud solutions. AWS Outposts helps organizations to run AWS services on-premises by providing them with infrastructure as a service in the form of AWS Outposts racks and servers. Organizations can run AWS services for computing, storage, etc., locally on their AWS Outposts hardware located on their premises and at the same time can access the AWS services in the region.

AWS Outposts is tied to the availability region where it is located, and AWS manages AWS Outposts instances as regional services. Hence, if we want to include outposts as part of a VPC, we can extend the VPC to AWS Outposts by creating an Outposts subnet.

Figure 7-3 shows the high-level architecture of AWS Outposts.

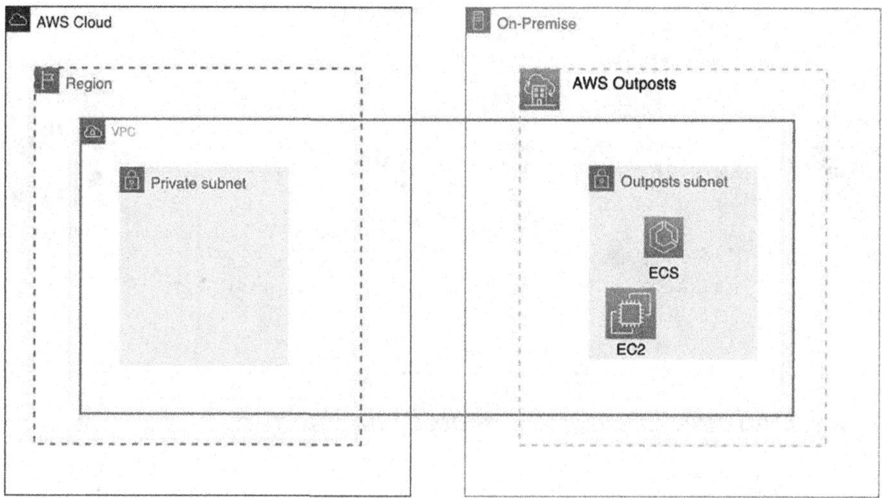


***Figure 7-3.*** *AWS Outposts high-level architecture*

The main disadvantage of AWS Outposts is that very few services are available on Outposts. As this book focuses mainly on serverless solutions, we won't discuss Outposts solutions in depth. However, keep in mind that we can also use AWS services on-premises even when we are proposing a hybrid cloud solution.

# Cloud-Agnostic Architecture

Nowadays, no enterprise wants to depend on a single cloud service provider while implementing solutions. They want to design their architectures in such a way that if they need to migrate their architecture to a new cloud service provider, they can do so with ease.

Cloud-agnostic architecture involves designing your application architecture in such a way that the services used in one cloud provider are available in other cloud providers as well, and they are easily portable. For example, if we are using Kubernetes to deploy the back-end application, then the back end can be easily migrated to other cloud providers as well, because Kubernetes is open source and is available on all major cloud platforms.

Let's look at a simple web application that is designed using the AWS cloud and yet uses a cloud-agnostic architecture. Figure 7-4 illustrates this architecture.

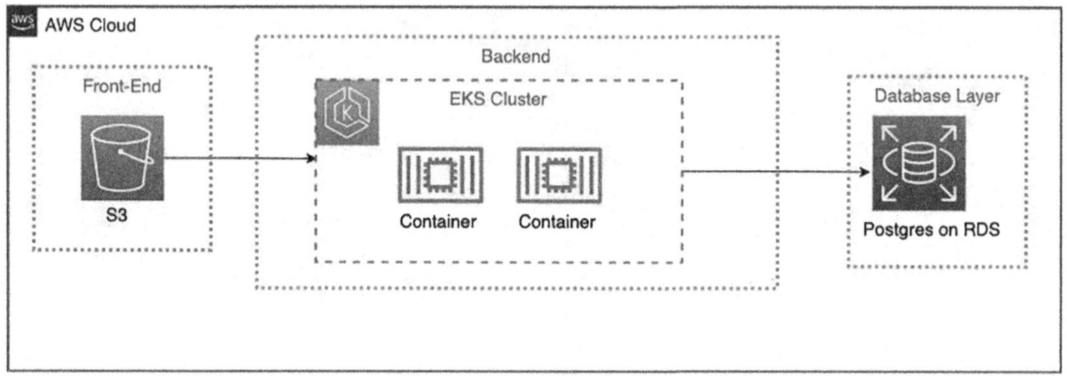


***Figure 7-4.*** *Cloud-specific yet cloud-agnostic architecture*

Now let's consider a scenario where the customer plans to migrate this application architecture from AWS to Azure.

The front end of this web application is hosted in S3, which contains static files such as HTML, CSS, JavaScript, and other static files. The front end can be downloaded via an S3 endpoint, and it can be uploaded to Azure within a few minutes. Just like S3, the object storage service in AWS, is used to host static website content, the same support is provided in Azure Storage.

The back end is hosted using containers that are orchestrated by the Elastic Kubernetes service, which is AWS. Since Kubernetes is open source and the container images are platform-independent and can be used to spin up containers in any environment, we can migrate them to Azure Kubernetes Services (AKS) or to Kubernetes clusters hosted in Azure virtual machines using the manifest files or helm charts that are used to set up Kubernetes clusters in AWS.

As the database is hosted in a PostgreSQL database using Amazon RDS, which is an open-source database and is available in Azure and most cloud platforms as well, it can easily be migrated to Azure DB for PostgreSQL using the Database Migration Service of Azure.

The source database can be kept online as well during the migration so that the application barely faces any downtime.

Now, let's see what the application architecture looks like post-migration to the Azure Cloud platform. Figure 7-5 shows the post-migration architecture.

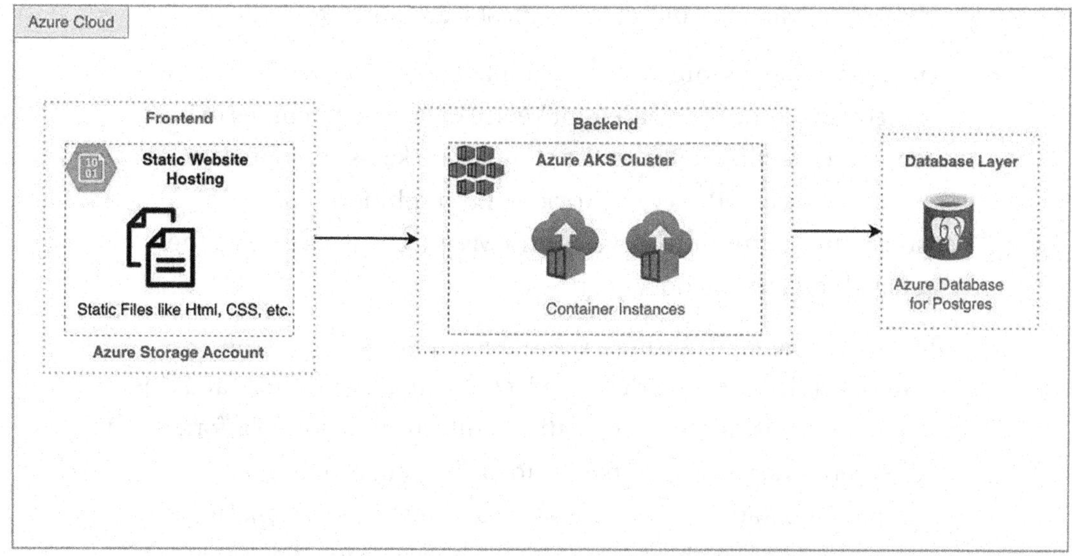


***Figure 7-5.*** *Cloud-agnostic architecture on Azure post-migration from AWS*

As we can see from Figure 7-5, it's comparatively easy to migrate an application from one cloud provider to another if it's designed in a cloud-agnostic manner. All you need to change is a few configurations and endpoints and the application can be up and running in minutes.

Here are the advantages of a cloud-agnostic architecture:

- *Ease of migration*: As we saw in the previous example of migrating from AWS to Azure, it just takes a few steps to migrate the application that is designed using cloud-agnostic architecture from one cloud provider to another. It is more like rehosting to a new platform.
- *No vendor lock-in*: As most services will be designed using open-source technologies, the application does not have a dependence on any single cloud provider, and the tech stack can be moved into another cloud provider with ease.
- *Less dependence on cloud-specific skills*: As the services being used in cloud-agnostic architectures are managed versions of the open-source technologies (like EKS is the managed version of Kubernetes), there aren't any provider-specific skills that are required to design such systems.

These are the disadvantages of a cloud-agnostic architecture:

- *Expensive*: When we are designing applications in a cloud-agnostic architecture, we need to either make use of virtual machines to host open-source technologies on the cloud or make use of managed services by the cloud service provider. Both solutions are not cost-effective as running services on VMs is a costly affair, and the managed services are not cheap.
- *Not always a good fit*: At times customers want to harness the platform services or serverless services for their application, and this is not possible using cloud-agnostic architecture as both platform and serverless services are specific to each cloud provider, and their implementation differs across cloud providers as well. Hence, customers will be unable to reap the benefits of using these services if they opt for cloud-agnostic architectures.

## Multicloud Architecture

In the past few years, *multicloud* is a term that has gotten a lot of traction at the enterprise level. Enterprises don't want to stick to a single cloud provider for their portfolio of applications; instead, they want to leverage the best from multiple cloud providers.

Multicloud architecture is the application architecture where multiple cloud providers are used to build a single application.

They can be purpose-driven as well, using the best services in each cloud to build their application platform. Based on the nature of implementation, multicloud architectures can be divided into two categories:

- *Distributed cloud architecture*: This means using the best-of-breed services across cloud providers to design your solution.
- *Polycloud architecture*: This means deploying the same solution across multiple clouds.

Now let's discuss these architectures in detail.

## Distributed Cloud Architecture

Each cloud provider has a service that is their hallmark service, and when designing solutions, architects across enterprises want to leverage these hallmark services and implement them in their solutions. Examples include Active Directory Service in Azure, the Kubernetes platform on Google, the Lambda FaaS on AWS, etc. This has led to a new solution paradigm of distributed multicloud architecture, or in short *multicloud.*

Let's consider an example. Suppose our customer wants to use all the services on AWS, but for the database, they want to use Azure, as they have a database cluster already running on Azure and they want to make use of it. This would be an ideal scenario for a distributed cloud architecture, as shown in Figure 7-6.

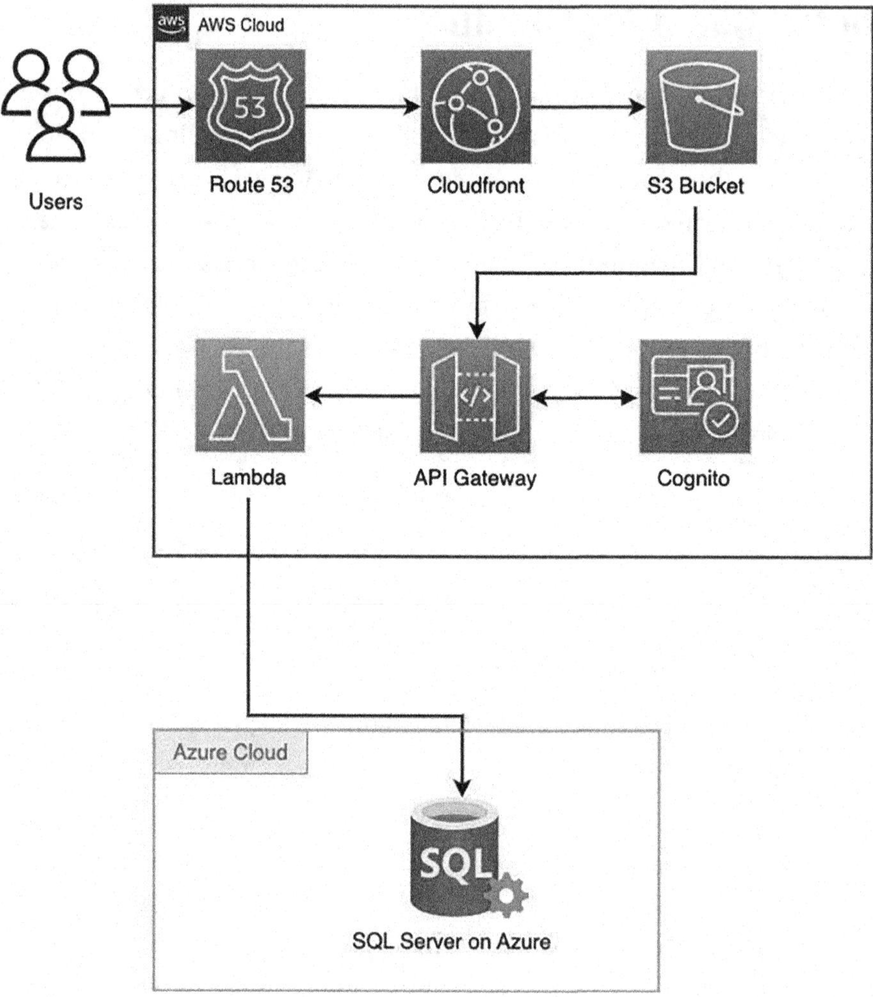


***Figure 7-6.*** *Distributed multicloud architecture*

As we can see from Figure 7-6, both Azure and AWS can co-exist with each other to deliver the distributed cloud architecture. One of the challenges in this type of architecture would be to reduce the latency due to the intercloud endpoint invocations. One of the ways to mitigate this would be to add a caching layer in AWS, or if the customer requires frequent writes to the database in Azure, then we need to use optimizing techniques in the database.

Distributed multicloud can extend to more than two clouds as well. Consider an example where we are using AWS, Azure, GCP, and Snowflake Cloud. The following is the overview of the architecture:

- The front end and CDN are hosted on the AWS cloud. We discussed these components in previous chapters, so I won't go in detail here.
- The authentication module is handled by the Azure cloud using the Active Directory service that is available on Azure.
- The back end follows a microservices architecture hosted on Google Cloud as containers utilizing the Google Kubernetes Engine for orchestration.
- For the database layer, Snowflake Data Cloud is used to host the databases.

See Figure 7-7.

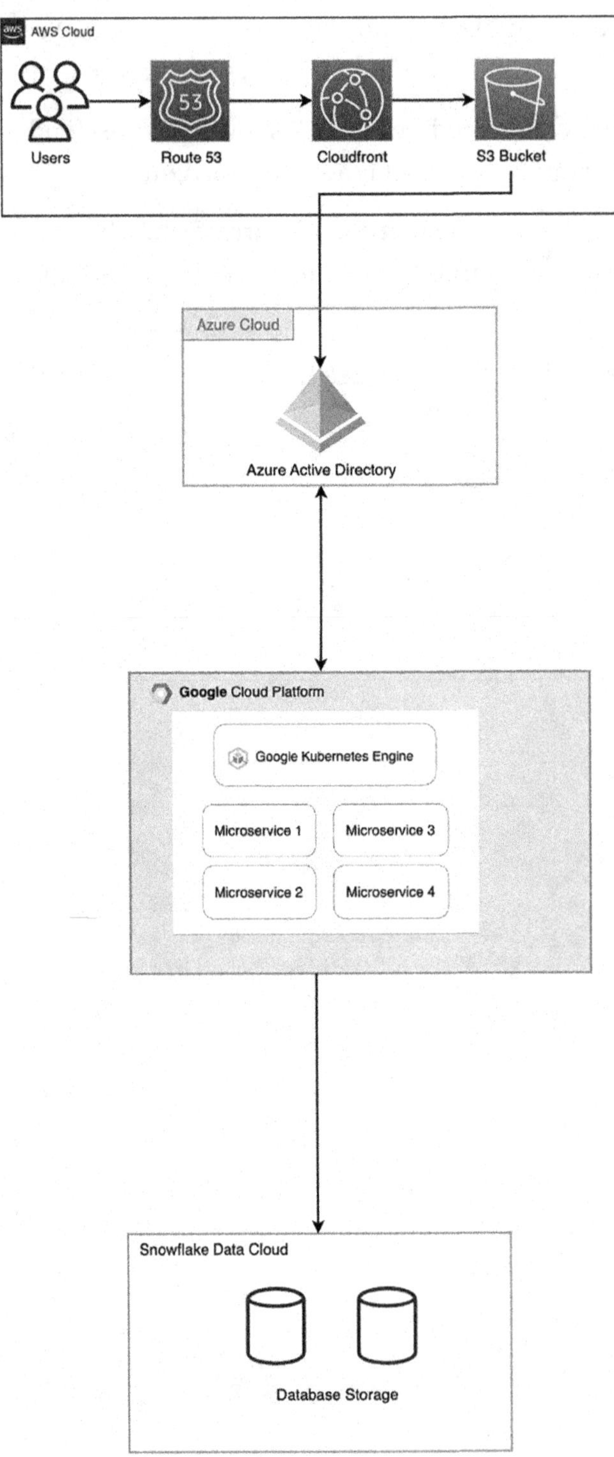


***Figure 7-7.** Distributed multicloud architecture*

## Polycloud Architecture

Enterprises often choose polycloud architectures to build resiliency into their existing systems. A *polycloud* architecture implies implementing the same system architecture across multiple cloud providers (generally two) to build resiliency or availability.

The architecture for polycloud is comparatively simpler in comparison to distributed cloud architecture. It has a traffic router, which would be a third-party implementation such as Megaport Cloud Router, and the Traffic Director would direct traffic based on any of the following commonly used conditions or a combination of one or more conditions:

- If Cloud Provider 1, the primary cloud, is not available, route to Cloud Provider 2.
- Depending on the latency of the region, route traffic to the cloud provider with the least latency.
- Divide the traffic equally among the cloud providers.

Note that these conditions are a few commonly used conditions, and there can be many more complex routing scenarios based on each customer's requirement. Figure 7-8 shows an example of a polycloud architecture.

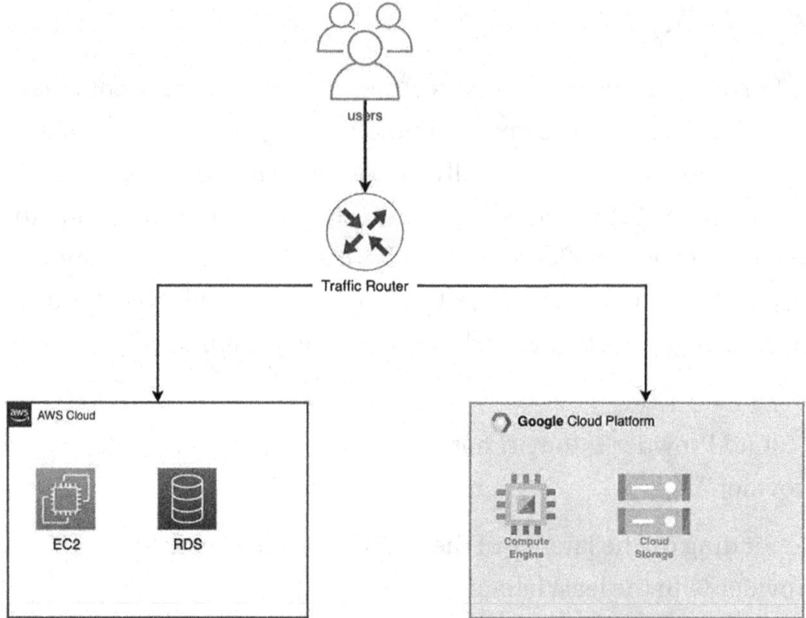


***Figure 7-8.*** *A polycloud implementation*

Now that we have familiarized ourselves with distributed clouds and polyclouds, let's compare the features of both in the following section.

## Distributed Cloud vs. Polycloud

Now that we have familiarized ourselves with two types of multicloud architectures, namely, distributed clouds and polyclouds, let's compare their features; see Table 7-1.

*Table 7-1. Distributed Cloud vs. Polycloud*

| Distributed Cloud | Polycloud |
|---|---|
| **Implementation** is complex as we need to integrate multiple services across cloud providers. | **Implementation** is simpler as we need to replicate the architecture in a completely new environment, and there are no complex cross-cloud provider integrations. |
| **Cheaper**, as we use only selected services from cloud providers. | **Costlier**, as the entire architecture including all services needs to be replicated. |
| **Latency is higher** as traffic needs to be routed across multiple services across cloud providers. | **Latency is lower**, as the only latency to be considered is that of the traffic router routing and once routed, all services exist in the same cloud provider and hence latency will be less. |
| **Less resilient** to cloud provider outages as the system can get impaired if one cloud provider faces an outage. | **Highly resilient** to cloud provider outages as even if one cloud provider faces an outage, another one is available to serve traffic. |
| **Difficult to monitor** as cloud services are spread across cloud providers and we need a third-party system to monitor the overall architecture. | **Easier to monitor**, as even though we leverage multiple cloud providers, the entire solution can be monitored separately under the respective cloud provider. |

# Comparison of Cloud Architectures

Now let's compare the cloud architectures based on the cost and implementation complexity. This is illustrated in Figure 7-9.

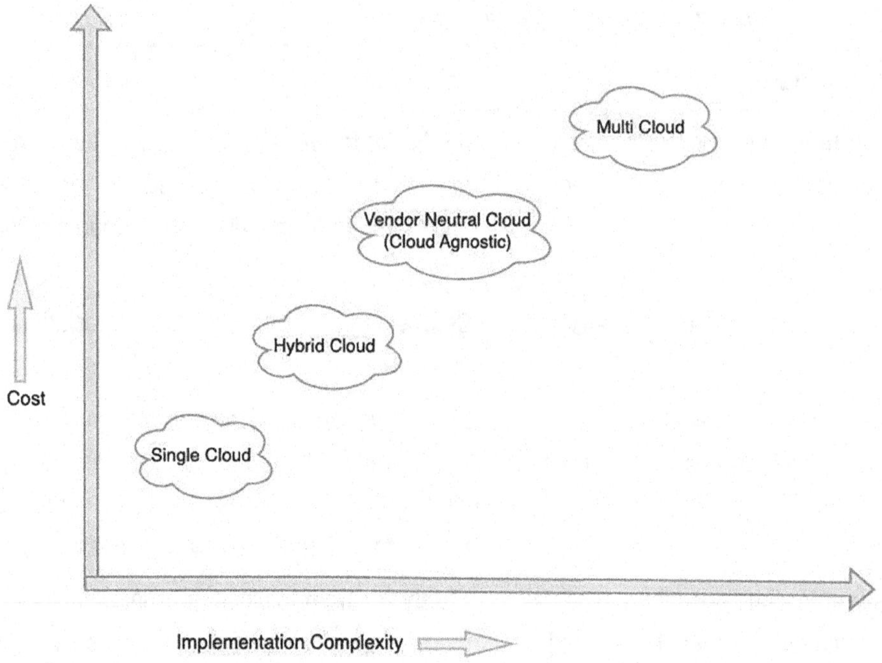


***Figure 7-9.*** *Comparison of cloud architectures*

As we can observe from Figure 7-9, designing a multicloud solution is a complex and costly affair. You should choose a multicloud solution if the business actually demands it, and if you are embarking on your cloud journey, it's always better to start simple with a single cloud provider as it would give you enough leeway to evaluate your workload and estimate the costs as well.

# Conclusion

In this chapter, we familiarized ourselves with the different types of cloud architectures and their pros and cons. We also learned in detail about different multicloud architectures with use cases. This brings us to the point where we need to evaluate the architectures based on the Well-Architected Framework tool provided by AWS. This is covered in detail in the next chapter.

# CHAPTER 8

# Serverless Through the AWS Well-Architected Framework

Throughout this book, we have explored different serverless architectures on AWS. AWS also provides developers with a framework called the AWS Well-Architected Framework that contains labs, tools, and lenses to evaluate workloads based on six pillars: operational excellence, security, reliability, performance efficiency, cost optimization, and sustainability.

In this chapter, we will do the following:

- Define the design principles for each pillar
- Evaluate the serverless architecture based on these six pillars
- Describe the steps to apply the Well-Architected Framework to architectures

## Operational Excellence Pillar

The operational excellence pillar deals with performing operations and processes to deliver business outcomes and constantly refine them.

The following are its design principles on the cloud.




J. J. Paul, *Distributed Serverless Architectures on AWS*, https://doi.org/10.1007/978-1-4842-9159-7_8

## Perform Operations As Code

This principle indicates the entire architecture should be designed as code, and there should be provisions to update it whenever required. The intent of this principle is to reduce human error and make the system responsive to events.

We utilized this design principle in Chapter 3, using Terraform to script the serverless web application, and the web application was event-driven as well. We can use any infrastructure-as-code tool to achieve this. Since most serverless services are event-driven, this design principle is inherently present in most serverless architectures. Figure 8-1 illustrates this principle.

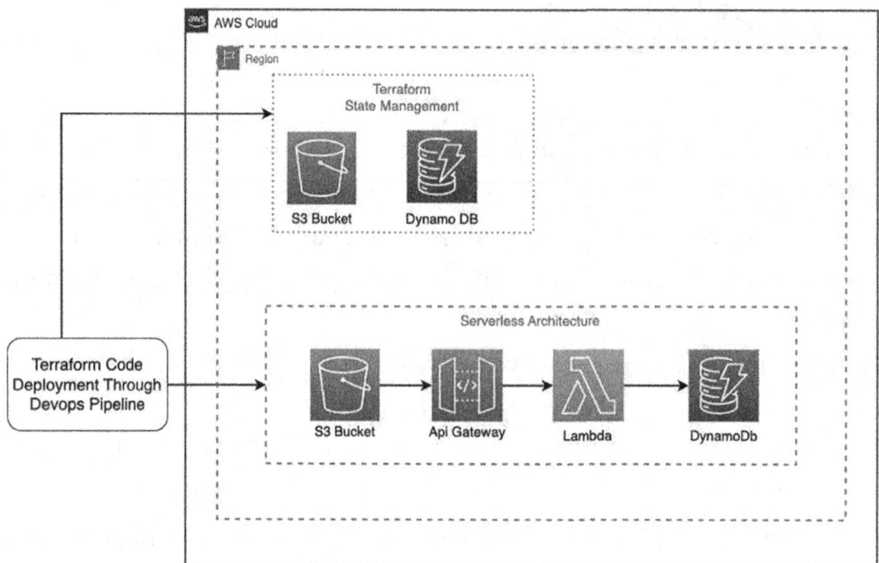


***Figure 8-1.*** *Performing operations as code using Terraform*

## Make Frequent, Small, Reversible Changes

This principle means that the changes that are applied can be done in isolation and if required rolled back as well.

As a follow-up to the first principle, this can be done using Terraform as well. We can write modules for individual components, thus making modular changes. We can do a `terraform destroy` and target the particular change that was implemented. The following is the syntax for the `terraform` command:

```
Terraform: Destroy Target Syntax
terraform destroy --target <<desired target>>
```

We discussed the Terraform code to implement a serverless web application in Chapter 3 (`https://github.com/jithinjudepaule/Distributed_Serverless_Architectures_Book/tree/main/TerraformSamples%20/Chapter3`). We can use the `terraform destroy` command to destroy or, rather, tear down this entire environment.

## Refine Operations Procedures Frequently

It is essential that the operations procedures set up for workloads are evaluated constantly. For example, if you have set up an operations procedure to evaluate the disaster recovery architecture for replication, recovery point objective (RPO), and recovery time objective (RTO) every month and you notice over a period of time that the RTO, RPO, and replication are as expected and there is hardly any change, then you can change the cadence from monthly to once every two months. But if the disaster recovery architecture is not performing as expected, then you can increase the cadence to biweekly.

It may not be possible to refine all operations regularly, but on a priority basis, we can target the necessary ones.

## Anticipate Failure

"Everything fails all the time" is the famous quote by Werner Vogels, Amazon's chief technology officer. So, it is essential that the systems we design should be resilient to failures. This also implies that we should make the systems highly available at both the availability zone level and the regional level. It is recommended that we perform these tasks way ahead of production by performing mock disaster or outage events. And they need to be resilient as well.

In serverless systems, these events can be carried out in a cost-effective way as the services are charged in a pay-per-use model. Hence, you incur charges only at the time of mocking the failure events.

## Learn from All Operational Failures

If any failures occur, derive patterns from them and create insights around them. Ensure that they are recorded in run books to ensure that they are not repeated during releases.

# Security Pillar

The security pillar describes best practices to make your cloud environment secure, respond to security events, and improve the overall security of your infrastructure on the cloud. The security pillar design principle applies across all services in AWS, and there are no specific principles for serverless workloads alone. Hence, what we cover in this section is applicable to all workloads on AWS.

The following are the design principles.

## Implement a Strong Identity Foundation

One of the foundations of identity management is the principle of least privilege, which implies that access to cloud services should be provided only to systems or users that need access.

In other words, systems or users should have access only to those systems that they use; granting access to anything beyond that is a potential threat.

In AWS, we use IAM to grant permissions to users and services. IAM is an account-wide service, and the permissions we set in IAM are accessible to all regions in the account. We make use of role-based access and add the services or users as trusted entities so that the principle of least privilege is followed. This is illustrated in Figure 8-2.

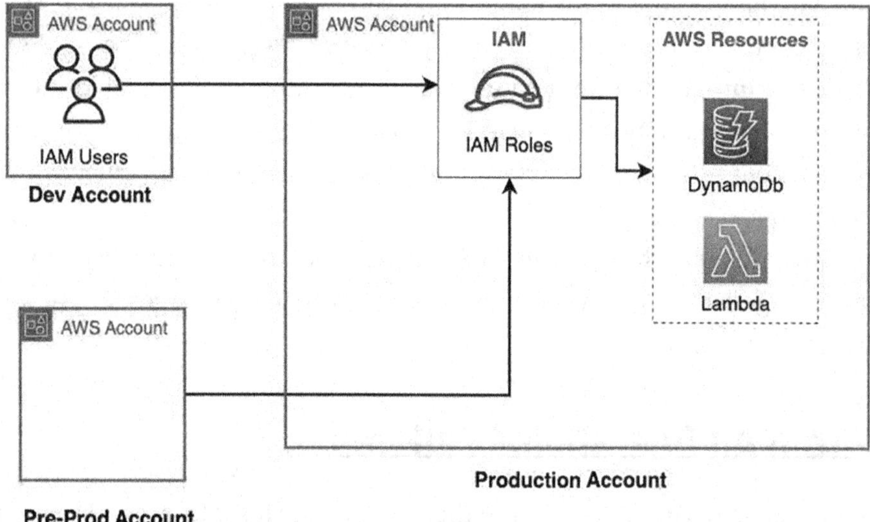


***Figure 8-2.*** *Role-based access*

If there is a need to centralize the permissions and enforce them across multiple accounts, we can make use of AWS Organizations, which enables us to create member accounts to a centralized root account and apply service control policies to the member accounts to define permission boundaries.

## Enable Traceability

It is quintessential while working with distributed systems to enable traceability at all layers of your application. Systems should be monitored, and automatic alerts should be kept at threshold levels that are agreed upon within the team. In the case of an alarm, the concerned team needs to be alerted using email or SMS. We can use the SNS service for this.

Also, the logs from all AWS services should be aggregated in the appropriate log groups so that in the case of an incident, the logs can be used to debug. To monitor all account-related activities on AWS, we can make use of the CloudTrail service.

## Automate Security Best Practices

This principle provides a defensive security practice where it is recommended to keep security at the center while designing architectures as well and to use automated software-based security mechanisms like Talisman (`https://thoughtworks.github.io/talisman/docs`), which is a repository hook and checks for potential SSH keys, authorization tokens, private keys, etc., in the outgoing changeset to the repository.

## Protect Data in Transit and at Rest

It is essential that we identify the PII data and encrypt it while persisting it in a persistent store. This will ensure that the data at rest is highly secure. We can use the AWS service KMS to achieve this and can use AWS Cloud HSM to harden it further.

For data protection in transit, AWS encrypts network traffic between AWS data centers. At the application layer, customers can use the Transport Layer Security (TLS) encryption protocol, and customers can upload their own digital certificates. Services such as AWS Load Balancer, API Gateway, etc., allow termination of TLS as well, and all service endpoints in AWS support TLS.

So, using AWS services such as KMS, CloudHSM and ACM customers can build a holistic data encryption strategy across their environments.

## Keep People Away from Data

To avoid mishandling data, it is always recommended to avoid direct access to data. This can be done by providing read-only access to developers, building a pipeline to deploy database changes, etc. Also, this principle ensures that manual processes are reduced and thus eliminates the errors due to the manual handling of data.

## Prepare for Security Events

Always anticipate security events such as DDOS attacks or ransomware attacks and ensure that there are incident management and other processes set up as per the customers' needs. Additionally, enabling the team to respond to security events by conducting mock attack scenarios will help the team be prepared in a better way for security events.

# Reliability Pillar

The reliability pillar deals with processes to make your workloads more reliable. The following are its design principles.

## Automatically Recover from Failure

This principle states that all workloads should be capable enough to automatically recover from failures. By setting key performance indicators (KPIs), monitoring them using monitoring services, and triggering automated recovery, this can be accomplished.

When working with serverless workloads on AWS, most of them recover automatically as the underlying hardware is managed by AWS. For example, if Lambda is not available to execute a function, then AWS spins up a new instance of Lambda and executes the function.

## Test Recovery Procedures

If we are setting up any recovery procedures, it is essential that we test them thoroughly before applying them to production workloads.

## Scale Horizontally to Increase Aggregate Workload Availability

To reduce single points of failure, it is better to keep the compute resources small and scale them horizontally on demand. We have followed this principle throughout the book, as we have designed the computing using Lambda for simple APIs and Fargate clusters for more connected and complex workloads.

## Stop Guessing Capacity

Scalability is one of the main advantages of cloud-based workloads over traditional on-premise workloads. The traffic coming into the workloads can be monitored, and the capacity can be decreased or increased dynamically.

## Manage Change in Automation

The changes made to the infrastructure should be in an automated manner. We can use pipelines to manage this change, and they can be audited through the state file of infrastructure-as-code tools like Terraform.

# Performance Efficiency Pillar

The performance efficiency pillar deals with the best practices for managing production workloads efficiently. The following are its design principles.

## Democratize Advanced Technologies

For teams to adopt the latest technologies, cloud providers ensure that these services are available as managed services. For example, for enterprises to adopt Kafka, AWS provides this as a managed service in the form of Amazon Managed Streaming for

Kafka (Amazon MSK). Another example is Elastic Kubernetes Service (EKS), which is the managed service from AWS for setting up Kubernetes on AWS. This principle recommends that the teams use such services from the cloud directly rather than learning the new technology and implementing it by themselves. This will enable organizations to focus more on the application rather than the infrastructure setup.

## Go Global in Minutes

This principle states that deploying the same application across multiple regions reduces latency and increases customer experience. This is easy to implement and cost-efficient as well using serverless technologies. We can keep a latency-based routing algorithm and serve traffic from the region with the lowest latency to users. This is illustrated in Figure 8-3.

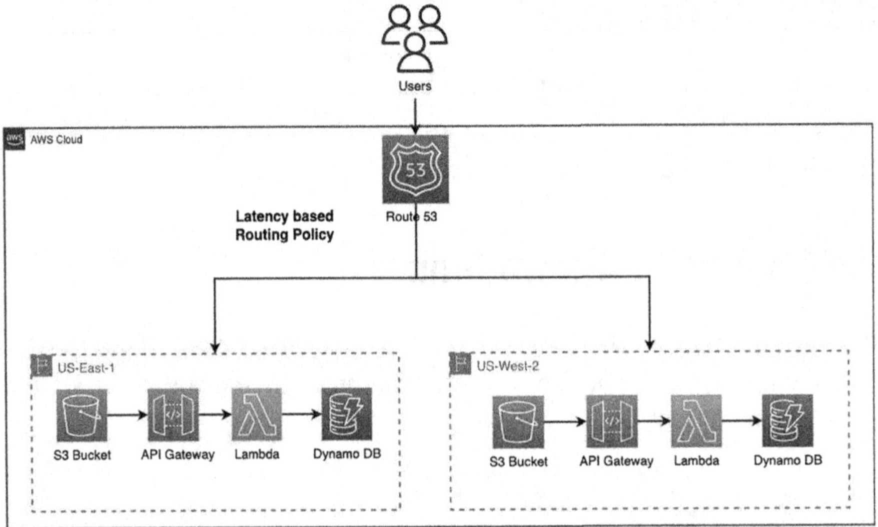


***Figure 8-3.*** *Latency-based routing across regions*

## Use Serverless Architectures

Serverless architectures eliminate the need for maintaining and provisioning physical servers. Hence, the compute gets managed by the cloud provider, and the experience is seamless. We have discussed serverless architectures at length throughout this book.

### Experiment More Often

As the pricing of cloud services is based on usage, it gives leeway for developers to experiment often and at the same time is inexpensive.

### Consider Mechanical Sympathy

Considering the apt technology for your business needs constitutes this design principle. There is no one-size-fits-all option when it comes to choosing your services. Evaluating your workload and its nature is essential before finalizing the technology stack for your business needs.

## Cost Optimization Pillar

The cost optimization pillar intends to bring down unnecessary costs and increase efficiency in the utilization of resources that are being paid for. The following are its design principles.

### Implement Cloud Financial Management

Even though there are multiple tools available in the market to evaluate the costs of running your environment on the cloud, there must be a dedicated team of individuals who manage cloud finances. This team can monitor the resources and report any kind of aberrations.

Setting up monthly and daily budgets is a way to monitor the costs incurred at regular intervals and can detect any anomalies arising due to a targeted attack or an unmonitored resource.

### Adopt a Consumption Model

When running applications against multiple environments like Dev, QA, etc., not all environments need to be up all the time. Organizations can come up with a consumption plan where they can decide when lesser used environments can be shut down and when they should be fully functional. This will lower the overall costs of multiple environments.

In the case of serverless workloads, this is taken care of, as they follow a pay-per-use model.

### Measure Overall Efficiency

The efficiency of your workloads can be measured by comparing them against the return on investment (ROI) as well as against the business objectives. Organizations can build data points around these objectives and decide on the areas they need to focus on to bring in more efficiency.

### Stop Spending Money on Undifferentiated Heavy Lifting

To focus more on building quality applications, it is always a good practice to offload the underlying hardware responsibilities to the cloud provider, which will in turn take care of the overall maintenance and monitoring of the servers on which the applications are hosted on the cloud. This enables organizations to deliver applications to market at a much faster rate. Serverless services are examples of services where the underlying hardware management is completely offloaded to the cloud provider.

### Analyze and Attribute Expenditure

The expenditures of different workloads across regions and accounts must be correctly classified into the respective teams or workloads. This will help organizations identify the investment areas and add or remove capacity to the required teams or workloads, respectively.

## Sustainability Pillar

The sustainability pillar in a nutshell involves design principles that will reduce the impact on the environment of running workloads on the cloud. It indicates the practices to be followed to reduce the carbon footprint while running workloads on the cloud.

Serverless is one of the best ways to implement a greener cloud in comparison to running systems on servers on the cloud, as serverless systems are utilized only for the duration they are accessed and the remaining time they are not running continuously, thus reducing the emissions from servers.

Also, serverless architectures run on shared hardware as most of the services are presented to the end users as a full service and they need to access them alone from their application. Such implementations will reduce the total number of servers required to run applications, thus reducing the carbon footprint and promoting a green cloud.

# Conclusion

In this chapter, we evaluated the design principles of the AWS Well-Architected Framework and compared them against the serverless design. You probably noticed that most of the design principles have been inherently applied to the serverless architectures that were discussed throughout this book. That brings us to a point where we can start thinking about what lies ahead of the serverless world. I will discuss that in the next chapter.

CHAPTER 9

# Looking Ahead

In this book, we introduced serverless and discussed serverless architectures for event-driven systems, disaster recovery systems, and more. This chapter focuses on what the future holds for serverless technologies.

## A Constantly Evolving Landscape

The serverless landscape of AWS is constantly evolving, and more and more services are being added to it every year. We saw that in the last few years even data platform services such as Elastic MapReduce have added a serverless flavor. In fact, even traditional database servers such as Postgres and MySQL and data warehousing services such as Redshift have serverless flavors available.

Because of this evolutionary nature of the serverless landscape, it is imperative to design systems with a serverless-first mindset as it will help to reduce costs drastically and offload the server management overhead. In the future, we can expect more enterprises to embrace this mindset.

## The Co-existence of Serverless Architectures

As the popularity of serverless is increasing, many enterprises will want to embrace serverless. While it is advantageous to design systems in a fully serverless manner, sometimes organizations are skeptical to fully embrace it because of the lack of control it brings as serverless services are fully managed services. This gives rise to a new paradigm that harnesses the best-of-breed serverless services and integrates them into their traditional architectures. This is a trend that is catching on quite fast among enterprises as it combines the benefits of serverless and brings forth the required controls as well.




J. J. Paul, *Distributed Serverless Architectures on AWS*, https://doi.org/10.1007/978-1-4842-9159-7_9

# Serverless Without Lambda

Ever since Lambda was launched by AWS in 2014, it has gained popularity worldwide, and it is difficult to imagine a serverless architecture without Lambda function. People have gotten so used to achieving integrations through Lambda that they overlook many of the native integrations that AWS services provide. For example, it is a common pattern to integrate API Gateway with the Lambda function, and the Lambda function will in turn connect with downstream services. But if we are utilizing Lambda from a purely integration perspective, we have other native integration options from API Gateway as well. Figure 9-1 shows the list of integrations that API Gateway provides to other services; this list is constantly being updated.

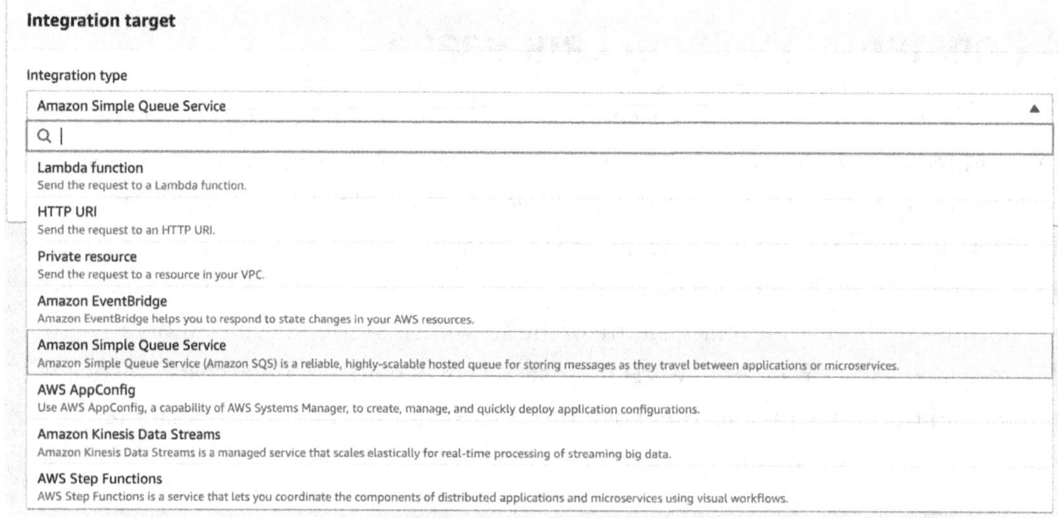


***Figure 9-1.*** *API Gateway integrations list*

By utilizing the AWS service integrations available through API Gateway, we can reduce the need for using Lambda functions as a mere service integrator and use it for more complex use cases.

# Driving the Growth Mindset

As serverless architectures are comparatively easy to set up when compared with their server-based counterparts and because they use a pay-per-use model, many organizations are using them as a base for their innovative workloads; this allows them to experiment with applications without worrying about the underlying hardware management. This enables enterprises to bring the ideas they invest to market within a short period of time. So, serverless is a forerunner for innovation and growth in any enterprise wanting to grow in the cloud ecosystem.

# Conclusion

The serverless landscape has a promising future, and if you are designing evolutionary architectures that are adaptable to future changes in the tech landscape, serverless is the way to go.

# Index


## A

Amazon Athena, 82, 84
Amazon Aurora Serverless, 7, 54
Amazon DynamoDb, 7, 28
Amazon EMR, 82
Amazon Event Bridge, 7
Amazon Kinesis, 34
Amazon Managed Streaming for Kafka (Amazon MSK), 137
Amazon QuickSight, 86, 88
Amazon RDS Proxy, 7
Amazon Redshift, 85
Amazon S3, 7, 79, 80, 86
Amazon Simple Notification Service (Amazon SNS), 7, 32, 39
Amazon SNS, 7
Amazon SQS, 4, 5, 7, 14, 15
API gateway, 7, 11, 27, 29, 54, 65, 67, 100, 135, 144
API management, 11
AppFlow service, 80
Aurora database, 45, 57
Aurora global database, 18
Automated software-based security mechanisms, 135
Availability zone, 49–52, 54, 133
AWS App2Container, 99
AWS AppRunner, 98
AWS AppSync, 7
AWS CloudFormation, 16, 28
AWS Cognito, 11
AWS components, 10
AWS data exchange, 79
AWS Data Pipeline service
- data import
  - DynamoDB, 92
  - verification, DynamoDB, 92
- data pipeline dashboard, 91
- DynamoDB export to S3, 90, 91
- DynamoDB table, data export, 89
- ETL service, 88
- export task configurations, 90
- import data, DynamoDB table, 89
- ready-to-use templates, 88

AWS DataSync, 79
AWS Fargate, 54, 98, 114
AWS Glue, 76, 77, 81, 82
AWS Lake Formation service, 80
AWS Lambda, 6, 16, 28, 98
AWS Outposts, 118, 119
AWS Red Hat OpenShift Service, 98
AWS S3, 11, 50, 76, 87
AWS serverless, 5, 7
AWS serverless ecosystem, containers, 97
- container hosting services, 98
- container modernization, 99
- container orchestration services, 97, 98
- container registry service, 98
- serverless web application, Fargate, 99–102

AWS SFTP, 80
AWS step functions, 7, 82





J. J. Paul, *Distributed Serverless Architectures on AWS*, https://doi.org/10.1007/978-1-4842-9159-7

AWS Well-Architected Framework
cost optimization pillar
adopt consumption model, 139, 140
analyze and attribute expenditure, 140
implement cloud financial management, 139
measure workloads efficiency, 140
undifferentiated heavy lifting, 140
operational excellence pillar
anticipate failure, 133
operational failures, 133
perform operations as code, 132
refine operations procedures, 133
terraform destroy, 132, 133
performance efficiency pillar
democratize advanced technologies, 137
latency-based routing algorithm, 138
mechanical sympathy, 139
use serverless architectures, 138
reliability pillar
automatic failure recovery, 136
capacity, 137
change management, automation, 137
scale horizontally to increase aggregate workload availability, 137
test recovery procedures, 137
security pillar
automate security best practices, 135
avoid mishandling data, 136
cloud environment, 134
data protection, transit, 135
design principle, 134
enable traceability, 135
identity management foundations, 134, 135
role-based access, 134
security events, 136
sustainability pillar, 140
Azure Kubernetes Services (AKS), 120

## B

Bounced email processor, 39
Bounced emails, 39–44

## C

Cloud-agnostic architecture
advantages, 121
AWS cloud, 119, 120
Azure post-migration, AWS, 121
disadvantages, 122
Kubernetes, 119
S3, 120
Cloud computing, 16
CloudFront service, 27, 52, 100
Container hosting services
AWS AppRunner, 98
AWS Fargate, 98
AWS Lambda, 98
Container modernization, 99
Container orchestration services
ECS, 97
EKS, 97
ROSA, 98
Container registry service, 98
Containers
AWS serverless ecosystem (*see* AWS serverless ecosystem, containers)
*runtime,* 95
*vs.* virtual machines, 95, 96

Cross-region disaster recovery strategy
AWS services, 58
back-end DR implementation
active-active configuration, 65, 66
custom domain mapping, API URLs, 66
route 53 domain mapping, 67
configuration, 58
failover policies, 58
front-end DR implementation, 60
create route 53 CNAME record failover routing policy, 64, 65
create S3 health check, 63, 64
destination bucket in AP-South-1, 63
IAM role, 60
replication rule configuration, S3 bucket, 62
S3 bucket, 59
Test data replication, US-East-1, 63
serverless, 59

## D

Database, 54, 55, 57, 58
Amazon SQS, 15
Aurora global database, 18
Aurora serverless database, 54
DR implementation, 67–71
migration service, 79
PostgreSQL, 120
relational, 7, 11
traditional, 143
Data consumption and visualization services
Amazon Athena, 84
Amazon QuickSight, 86
Amazon Redshift, 85
Data ingestion services, 76
AWS data exchange, 79
AWS DataSync, 79
database migration service, 79
Kinesis Data Firehose, 79
Data platforms, 93, 143
advantages, cloud, 77
data ingestion, 76
data processing, 76
data storage, 76
data visualization, 76
end-to-end solution, 75
high level, 75
Data processing services, 76
Amazon Athena, 82
Amazon EMR, 82
AWS Glue, 81
AWS step functions, 82
EMR cluster creation, 84
EMR cluster creation, step functions service, 83
step functions flow visualization, 83
Data replication, 63, 69, 70
Data storage services, 76, 80
Data visualization, 76, 88
Democratize advanced technologies, 137–138
Disaster recovery (DR) architectures, 13, 20–21, 49–73
Disaster recovery strategies
region
cross-region, 58–67
database DR implementation, 67, 69, 71
geographic topology, AWS cloud, 50, 52
multi-AZ disaster recovery strategy, 52–56, 58

Disaster recovery strategies (*cont.*)
RTO and RPO
active-active configuration, 73
active backups only, 72
active-passive configuration, 73
dashboard, AWS Backup service, 72
Distributed cloud architecture, 123–126
Distributed system, 14
architectural patterns
DR architecture, 20, 21
event-driven architecture, 19, 20
cloud computing, 16
fault tolerant, 15
highly available, 16
immutable architecture, 16
near-zero latency, 14, 15
orchestrating actions, 17, 18
scalability, 16
SQS, 15
DynamoDB, 11, 28, 29, 32, 39, 41, 67, 71, 76, 91–93
DynamoDB table, 34, 40, 67, 68, 89

## E

ECSFargateCluster, 107
Elastic Container Registry (ECR), 98–99, 104, 112, 113
Elastic Kubernetes Service (EKS), 6, 54, 97, 99, 103, 120, 121, 138
Emailing Service with bounced email
add Lambda Subscriber, 40
add subscriber, 41
Aurora database, 45
AWS service limits, 39
bounced email logs, CloudWatch, 42, 43
bounce rate, 39
create event subscription, RDS, 46
create SNS topic, 39
enable bounce email notification, SES, 40, 41
Lambda function, 38
notifications, RDS instance, 47
RDS event subscriptions, 45
setting up test email, 42
SNS topic, 47
workflow, bounced email detection, 44
Event, 23, 45
consumer, 26
processor, 25
producer, 24
trigger, 24, 25
Event-driven architectures, 19, 20
anatomy, 23
event consumer, 26
event processor, 25
event producer, 24
event trigger, 24, 25
monitor and alert, 45
streaming event processor, 34–38

## F

Fargate, 6, 97–110, 114, 137
Fault tolerant, 15, 19, 51
Fully managed service, 3
Apache Kafka service, 3, 4
Function-as-a-service (FaaS), 1, 6, 10, 11, 28

## G

Geographic topology, AWS cloud, 50
availability zone, 50, 51
regions, 51

VPC and subnet CIDR ranges,
region, 51
Global distributed apps
advantages, 19
disadvantages, 19
GraphQL APIs, 7
Greener cloud, 140

## H

High-level event-driven system, 20
Hybrid cloud architecture
advantages, 117
AWS, 117
AWS Outposts, 118, 119
disadvantages, 118
organizations, 116

## I, J

Immutable architecture, 16
Internet, 13

## K

Key performance indicators
(KPIs), 136
Kinesis Data Firehose, 79, 87
Kinesis Streams, 34, 35
Kubernetes, 97, 119–121, 123

## L

Lambda, 10, 11, 28
Lambda function, 36
serverless architecture, 144
s3-event-processor, 26
SQS trigger, 33
Lambda test event, 38
Latency-based routing algorithm, 138

## M

Multi-AZ disaster recovery strategy, 53
Aurora database cluster view, 57
Aurora multi-AZ configuration, 55
back end, 54
database, 54, 55, 57, 58
front end, 53
Triggering failover, 57
Multicloud architecture
categories, 122
distributed cloud architecture, 123–126
distributed cloud *vs.* polycloud, 129
polycloud architectures, 127, 128

## N, O

Near-zero latency, 14, 15
Network File System (NFS), 79
NoSQL database, 11

## P

Pay-per-use model, 4, 9, 133, 140, 144
Polycloud architectures
conditions, 127
distributed cloud *vs.* polycloud,
128, 129
implementation, 128
PostgreSQL database, 120
Private network service, 116

## Q

QuickSight, 76, 86, 88

## R

Real-time processing systems, 16
Recovery point objective (RPO), 20, 49, 71–73, 133
Recovery time objective (RTO), 20, 49, 71–73, 133
Red Hat OpenShift Service on AWS (ROSA), 98
Regions, 17–19, 49–52, 58, 59, 66, 67, 72, 73, 77, 134, 138, 140
Replica table, 67–69
Replication rule configuration
  S3, 60
  S3 bucket, 62
Resilient event-driven application, 32
Resilient serverless web application
  Amazon SNS, 32
  SQS, 32, 33
REST APIs, 7, 27, 28
Return on investment (ROI), 140

## S

S3 bucket, 15, 17, 25, 27, 59, 62–65, 79, 80, 89
S3 event trigger, Lambda function, 25
Scalability, 11, 16, 77, 137
Self-managed services, 2, 3
Serverless architectures, 1, 9–11, 52, 59, 71, 73, 131, 132, 138, 141, 143
  API Gateway integrations list, 144
  Lambda function, 144
  pay-per-use model, 144
Serverless container services, AWS
  run containers on Fargate
    Browser output, hosted app, 108
    create cluster, 104
    create ECS cluster, 103
    deploy service with tasks, 105
    load balancing configuration, 106, 107
    service deployment, 106
    task definition creation, 104
    task revision option, 109
    tasks status, 107
    task status update after revision, 110
  run containers on Lambda
    build image, 112
    create Lambda function, 111
    create Lambda function with image, 113
    host container images, 111
    log in to ECR via Terminal, 112
    package Lambda function, image, 112
    tag and push image, 113
    test Lambda function, 113, 114
Serverless data analytics application, 87, 88
Serverless data platform on AWS, 78
  Amazon AppFlow, 80
  AWS SFTP, 80
  data consumption and visualization services, 84–86
  data ingestion services, 78–80
  data processing services, 81–84
  data storage services, 80
Serverless-first mindset, 9, 10, 143
Serverless landscape, AWS, 143, 145
Serverless pattern, 1, 9
Serverless services, 140
  abstraction levels vs. application code focus, tech stacks, 8
  Amazon SQS, 4, 5
  advantages, 9

application integration, 7
compute
AWS Lambda, 6
the Fargate service, 6
data store, 7
distributed batch processing, 17
FaaS, 10, 11
fully managed services, 4
list of AWS services, 5, 6
pay-per-use model, 4
SQS, 4
Serverless technology
FaaS, 1
serverless patterns, 1, 2
Serverless web application, 27
API Gateway, 27
AWS, 27
CloudFront service, 27
DynamoDB, 28, 29
Lambda, 28
resilient, 31–33
S3 bucket, 27
Terraform output, Lambda module, 29
Serverless web application, Fargate, 100
APIs, 100
cluster, 100
cluster dashboard, 101
ECS, 100
front end, 100
service, 102
task, 102
task definition, 101
task definition configuration, 102
Server Message Block (SMB), 79
Service autoscaling, 106
Simple Queue Service (SQS), 4, 5, 14, 15, 32–33
Single-cloud architecture, 116
advantages, 116
cloud-based architectures, 115
disadvantages, 116
SQS queue, 33
Streaming event processor, 34–38


## T


Talisman, 135
Task definition, 101, 102, 104, 105, 108
Terraform, 16, 28, 132, 137
TestTable, 89
The Amazon API Gateway, 7
The Fargate service, 6
Transport Layer Security (TLS), 135
Types of cloud architectures
cloud-agnostic architecture, 119–122
comparison, 129, 130
hybrid cloud architecture, 116–119
multicloud architecture (*see* Multicloud architecture)
single-cloud architecture, 115, 116


## U


User-managed services, 2


## V


Virtual machines, 2, 95, 96, 99, 116, 120, 122
VPN, 116


## W, X, Y, Z


WebSocket APIs, 11, 27

Printed in the United States
by Baker & Taylor Publisher Services